TRUE STORIES OF THE STRANGE AND UNUSUAL

Book 1

DE FLETCHER

Spirit Oaks
PRESS

Copyright © 2025 by De Fletcher. All rights reserved. Visit the author's website at MyParanormalStories.com

No portion of this book may be reproduced in any form without written permission from the publisher or author, except as permitted by United States copyright law.

The publisher of this book does not authorize the use or reproduction of any part of this book in any manner for the purpose of training artificial intelligence (AI) technologies or systems. The publisher of this book expressly reserves this book from the Text and Data Mining exception in accordance with Article 4(3) of the European Union Digital Single Market Directive 2019/790.

ISBN: 978-1-7379507-7-6 (Paperback)

Edited by ProofProfessor

Book cover by 100 Covers

First edition 2025

To Vandra Morgan-Delaney.
Thank you for your friendship and spiritual insights.

"The world is full of magic things, patiently waiting for our senses to grow sharper."

-William Butler Yeats, Irish poet, 1865-1939

Contents

Preface i

1	Whispers in Print 1	
2	The Murder of Crows 9	
3	Psycho Smoking Cessation 15	
4	Murdered in Mena 21	
5	Dental Delirium 27	
6	No Good Will Come of This 33	
7	Slo-Mo 18-Wheeler 43	
8	Missing Kentucky Mom 51	
9	Death From the Inside Out 57	
10	The Flashing Red Number 3 67	
11	A Chance Call 73	
12	Forgotten Father 81	

Contents (2)

13	Places of Healing	89
14	An Amber Alert	97
15	The Vietnam Veterans Memorial	105
16	Who Killed Kenny?	111
17	Encased in the Embankment	121
18	Capitol at Seventh	129
19	Life's Memories Lost	133
20	The Sorrow of the Red Stone	143

Can't Wait for Book 2? 153

Also by De Fletcher 155

About the Author 159

Coming Soon 161

Acknowledgements 163

Before You Read This Book

This publication contains stories of crime, death, and other paranormal events that are graphic in nature. Reader discretion is advised.

Every effort has been made to ensure details are presented in a manner that removes any inclination toward being graphic for mere shock value.

The identities of persons, family members, and other parties have been omitted out of respect for their privacy. Any details or other information shared about particular events are alleged and are inadmissible in a court of law.

Preface

As a child, I knew things far beyond my years. I could sense things others didn't and hear whispers guiding me to know right from wrong. I couldn't tell you how I knew, I just did. These "knowings" operated like some sort of built-in navigation system. Whispers of places not to go, knowing when people were being deceptive, and good (or bad) feelings about people or places. My attention would focus on things others didn't notice, oftentimes hearing or seeing things that others didn't. My family didn't believe in this sort of stuff, so it became abundantly clear this type of behavior was not acceptable. So, I was trained to do what was expected and acceptable in "normal" society and silence the other part of my being.

Over the years, brief moments of this guidance would pop up from time to time. Usually, the clarity would hit me when I was in danger or at a low point in life. I realized then that the help I'd received as a child hadn't really gone away. It was still there . . . waiting for me to use it again!

After an epiphany experience in my early thirties, I spent years reawakening my abilities. Then came a profound experience with a magazine (of all things), which gave me a glimpse into all that was possible if I chose to trust my inner guidance again.

A quadruple homicide and an Amber Alert soon followed. They helped strengthen my spiritual muscles even more. These types of events have increased in frequency to the point of becoming almost everyday occurrences!

I've had experiences most people would not believe, like seeing a mountain cry, the Earth breathing, and feeling the presence of the Angel of Death right before a loved one crossed over. Deceased relatives have come to deliver birthday greetings and I've witnessed my ancestors lining up to greet a relative as they were crossing over. There have been many more, but these are just a few that come to mind.

Understanding the language I use in this book to describe how I receive the paranormal information will help you feel the full impact of the stories. The information I receive comes through my physical senses. Normally, I get a heads-up just before I'm hit with incoming insights. The hair on the back of my neck may stand on end, a chill might run down my spine, or I'll actually feel a change in the environment (cold, stillness, wind, sounds, and more). Sometimes a person, place, or event comes into my awareness multiple times (getting my attention). In these cases, I'll usually say, "It came to me."

In other instances I physically feel time slowing down, view the "happening" in slow-motion, then time will return to normal. For those events I say, "Time slowed down". Most of the time I will describe which of my senses picked up the information (heard, saw, felt, smelled, or tasted). There have also been experiences where my environment becomes utterly silent right before I receive a message. In those instances, I refer to it as "the silence". Frequently, I'll see a snapshot or short video (like a TikTok) in my mind's eye (like when we imagine).

Over the ages, there have been many terms used to describe people who have ESP (extrasensory perception) or a sixth sense. Seer, witness, medium, psychic, fortune-teller, channel, and oracle are some that come to mind. I prefer to refer to myself as a spiritual conduit, but if I had to otherwise label myself, I'd probably begrudgingly settle for psychic medium. My inherent spiritual gifts are plugged into what I call "Source" or spiritual frequency.

The stories in this book are written in the storyteller style. Each begins with the backstory, then reveals how/why my psychic gifts were activated, and then details the paranormal experience that came with each mystery or death, or just going-about-my-day stuff.

Within these pages, I share with you the strange, dark, and mysterious stories of my life as a psychic medium. Some are creepy, scary, and heart-pounding. Others are sad, illuminating, embarrassing, and everything in between.

I think it's only fitting to begin with the event that showed me (in a big way) that my spiritual abilities had indeed reawakened. This out-of-the-blue experience would change my life path trajectory. How was I to know reading a magazine article would become a life-altering event?

1
Whispers in Print

Not long after settling into my second home, my childhood "knowings" started coming back. At first, random events happened that didn't seem to be caused by anything in particular. As time went on, the type and frequency of these events increased. Within a year, my hearing, seeing, knowing, and even smelling things others did not became commonplace. All those quick flashes of information and video "shorts" ended on a sultry, August afternoon.

Relaxing on the porch, I decided to read the latest edition of a local publication (*AY Magazine*). After glancing at its contents, I turned to a section of interest titled *Murder Mystery*. The article was about *Lives Lost & Found*. It summarized a few of the oldest unsolved cases of unidentified persons in Arkansas.

My own experience with missing family members had sparked my interest in cold cases decades before.

Settling into my comfy chair, I started reading the first unidentified summary. A feeling of genuine sadness for the person they described came over me. His remains were discovered in 1978, floating face-down in a creek. His hands were tied together at the wrists and affixed to the ankles, which were also tied together. Since his body was found in a state of advanced decomposition, facial identification wasn't possible. The only identifying evidence left was his dental work, a heart tattoo on his right arm, and the clothing he had on when he died. Back in 1978, DNA technology wasn't available, so his remains were cremated and buried, closing the door on any future testing.

After finishing the article, my mind tried to imagine how his loved ones must have felt. Their son, brother, or father seemingly vanishing without a trace. Suddenly, in the midst of my mental meanderings, I heard a name! "What the heck was that?" I asked myself. Why a name had popped into my head I didn't know . . . couldn't explain. No, it hadn't popped into my head . . . I had heard it! Just as the last thought left my brain, I heard the same name again! In an instant, my creep-out meter went from confusion to holy sh*t!

That feeling you get when you know something otherworldly is going on and you're not sure your mind can handle it.

To regain some sense of calm, I told myself there was no way a guy who had been murdered so long ago could have whispered his name to me. No one knew his name, where he was from, or who had left him in that creek. My logic tried desperately to dismiss what I'd clearly heard.

Still feeling a little unnerved, I hesitated for a bit before deciding to continue reading the article. The second case summary was of a petite woman's partial skeletal remains found discarded alongside railroad tracks in 1994. No fingerprints or facial recognition was possible, but authorities were able to extract her DNA. They were also able to get a description of the woman based on her remains. She was still wearing the clothes she wore on the day she died. Her dental work rounded out the last of the evidence.

Once I had finished reading about this small woman who was dumped like trash near a rural town, my mind started going over the evidence. Law enforcement had her description, DNA, and a very unique T-shirt she had been wearing. Why haven't they solved this case? Just as I finished those thoughts . . . I heard another name!

Immediately, my creep-out meter went off the scale. My hair stood on end and chills (like cold lightning) went up my spine. The name had been a female name. Two different names. Two different stories. Two different genders. What I was experiencing was officially no longer a one-off. Gingerly, I wrote each name I'd heard next to their respective summary. At this point, my curiosity wouldn't allow me to close the magazine and ignore the next summary. Would it happen a third time?

Nothing I had read so far prepared me for the gruesomeness of the third summary. Back in 1970, somebody decided to go looking for poke (poke salad) up on the highest peak in Arkansas. What the person came upon instead was the headless, partial torso of a man. The torso had been severed just above the navel with the legs cut off just above the knees. It was observed sitting upright on a tree stump (like it had been put on display).

The man's head was missing, as were his arms and the upper portion of his torso. The legs that had been cut off just above the knees were also missing. The day after the initial horrifying discovery, a search party found five bloody, black plastic bags with a trademark green leaf on them.

One of the bags held human hair, another contained intestines, and the other bags had been torn and emptied by animals. The rest of the body was never located.

The only clues law enforcement had in this case was that the victim was a white male of unknown age with light brown and gray pubic hair. Again, I went over what was known about this murder in my mind. It seemed whoever had killed and dismembered this man had made sure no identifying parts would be found. Maybe that was the whole point (beyond displaying the torso). In all likelihood, the man had tattoos, piercings, birthmarks, or other identifying items on his body.

Perhaps my expecting a third name was the reason no name came to me for this case. This outcome was very disappointing (considering what I had received for the other cases). Why wouldn't I get a name for this person as well? Was his identity to remain a mystery forever? Then, in my mind's eye, came a living photo! (A living photo is a photo where the objects or people in the photo are alive. They move around, look directly at you, or sometimes talk.) This man wasn't talking to me, but I could clearly tell he was alive. The photo was a waist-up shot. His torso was shirtless and intact, his head still on his body.

Immediately, I knew <u>he was showing me what his killer had successfully erased</u>!

The hobo spider tattoo started on his left chest and its web stretched upward and outward to his neck and jaw. It was large and distinctive. Anyone who knew him would have recognized such a tattoo. It appeared somewhat faded from age, wasn't a professional tattoo, and probably wasn't done in one sitting. He also seemed to have another tattoo on his right upper arm, though I couldn't see the image (just the edges of ink). The man I saw had a light complexion, medium brown hair, and brown eyes. He appeared to be in his mid-to-late thirties or early forties.

There's no doubt in my mind that I heard the names and saw the very people I was reading about. It was as if someone had been there while I was reading, waiting for me to finish each story before telling me **who** the story was about! In my state of shock (or disbelief) I didn't know what to do with the information I'd received. I let it simmer for a few days, but what to do still eluded me. If I had shared this with anyone (at the time), it may have helped me figure out what to do, but I was afraid of ridicule if someone asked me HOW I came across the information.

Finally, I tore the article from the magazine and put it on my bookshelf. Time passed, and the article got buried beneath other papers, but I never threw it away. Each time I cleaned off the bookshelf, I would keep the article. More time passed, spiritual experiences kept happening, and I put the article away in my filing cabinet. I don't think I passed along the information I had received while reading the *AY Magazine* article to law enforcement, but I did submit a possible match to NamUs (a database for the missing and unidentified).

All three unidentified remains cases remain unsolved.

2
The Murder of Crows

Superstitions abound in our human world. Some are as old as the country from which they originated. Also known as omens or signs, they are passed down through generations of families. These omens can be about people, places, things, animals, certain names, forbidden words, and more. Some people believe owls are a harbinger of death, storks are a sign of a new birth, horses represent freedom (breaking loose of the things that bind us), black cats are bad luck, and snakes are indicative of evil works in the making. Some cultures tell us to pay attention when an animal is acting out of character. That it's a personal message for us. These cultures remind their people that they should always pay attention (and heed) these omens or superstitions . . . if they know what's good for them.

My omen experience involved crows.

It was a cloudy, rain-drizzled day at work. A couple of colleagues and I went outside for a smoke break to satisfy our nicotine cravings. Within a few minutes, a flock of crows (known as a "murder") flew in and landed in the trees all around us. They started cawing very loudly. Now, this isn't unusual in itself. A murder of crows will often fly into an area, cover the surrounding trees with their shiny black feathers, and talk (caw) amongst themselves. After a while, they will take off (almost in unison) to fly to another location, looking like a swarm, swaying to and fro. We finished our smokes and returned to work.

A few hours later, we returned to our smoke spot and the crows were still in the trees. Maybe they had flown off and returned later, but from our point of view they hadn't moved from their previous perches among the trees. We each remarked about this and how it was kind of strange. Their caws had increased in volume as well. So much so that we cut our break short and went back to work. Our afternoon break was a repeat of our previous two outings, except this time it seemed (at least to me) that every single crow had started cawing at the same time. The sound was so loud that they were clearly heard from inside the building!

It was at this point that my colleagues and I remarked that we'd never experienced this level of crow activity, and it was starting to creep us out a bit. One person remarked that the crows would be gone by the next day. So, our workday ended and we headed home to do whatever we do before we sleep and then wake to do it all over again.

On the second day the weather was still overcast, cool, and rainy. When we arrived for work, the crows had not left. It didn't even appear that their numbers had decreased! At first break, the smokers decided to go to a different area of the parking lot with fewer trees. It didn't help the noise level much. The crows were still at it. All of them were "talking" loudly at once. It reminded me of people in a verbal argument, where each one is talking over the other, and the volume of their voices keeps rising the longer the disagreement goes on. Again, the cawing was so loud we could hear it plainly inside our workplace! It was almost as if the crows were inside the building.

By the end of day two, most of my co-workers had a sense of dread from the crows who were just hanging around and acting weird. Maybe the signs/omens stories they were told as children kicked in.

Perhaps it was the weather of cold, gray, rain, and intermittent fog that was also plaguing the area that made the ominous feeling more palatable. Some of the crows even perched on the lower branches of the trees. Low enough to see their faces (and look into their dark obsidian eyes) as they looked directly at me, cawing over and over at an unrelenting pace.

At this point, I felt like screaming out, "What?!" in the hope I would get some reply, and the murder would finally move on. I received no reply and the murder stayed. The ongoing noise, weather, and behavior of the crows were quite unnerving. The whole experience was weird, reminiscent of a macabre setting in a story penned by Poe, and so unlike any experience I'd ever had with crows.

After the third day, the crows moved on. The weather brought sunshine and blue skies. The overall sense of strangeness cleared up as well. Colleagues breathed a sigh of relief, happy to be finally free of the noise, depressive weather, and constant sprinkling of rain. Everyone was glad to no longer hear the loud, incessant caws hour after hour, day after day. But, in the back of our minds, everyone wondered what the crows' extended visit meant.

Some cultures believe the crow is a messenger that brings warnings. Others say if the crow talks to you, you should listen. If you don't, you do so at your own peril. Perhaps crows give us a heads-up, so we proceed with caution. Maybe their forewarnings are to help us prepare for what is coming. Although I didn't recognize it at the time . . . the crows in the trees were trying to prepare me for the knock upon my door that was forthcoming . . . one that plunged me into the darkest period of my life.

A week or so later, I was talking to my sister on the phone when my doorbell rang. I put the phone down and answer the door. My sister-in-law was standing on the porch. I was happy to see her and smiled, but noticed she wasn't smiling back. She had a strange look on her face (and I noticed my niece had stayed in their car). I think I asked her what was wrong. She told me my elder brother had found my younger brother unresponsive at his house earlier that afternoon. The paramedics had pronounced him dead at the scene.

An involuntary scream of anguish left my mouth, my knees buckled, and I fell to the floor sobbing. Forgetting all about my sister who was still on the phone . . . hearing my pain-filled scream. My fiancé came running into the room in a panic, wondering what was going on.

My sister-in-law got on the phone with my younger sister and told her what had happened. I don't remember talking to my sister again that day. In a single moment . . . having never gone to sleep . . . I woke up in the middle of a bad dream.

My brother and I had just gone out for lunch earlier that month! The day had been nice with sun and blue skies. I was happy to spend some time with him. Our lunch went way past my allotted hour, so I rushed back to work. He came into the building with me and we chatted in the foyer for a few more minutes. As he was leaving, he gave me one of his famous bear-hugs (although much tighter than usual). Then he said, "I love you, sis." I knew he meant those words! I told him, "I love you, too, bro," and I meant every word! After he left, I went back to my desk amongst a sea of cubicles.

It was almost like he didn't want our time to end. It's one of those things that comes to mind later (like flashbacks in slow motion) and you kick yourself for not having noticed. Turns out that our lunch that day was the first sign I didn't recognize. The second being the murder of crows.

Our lunch that day would be the last time I saw my brother.

3
Psycho Smoking Cessation

If anyone ever tells you that quitting smoking is hard . . . believe them!

My love/hate relationship with cigarettes began in junior high school. It may be a story that's been told a thousand times, but it started with a puff or two in the girls' bathroom. Sneaking a smoke without getting caught was a rebel thing to do back then. That drag or two once or twice a week slowly progressed to every day, then to half a cigarette, then full ones. Trying to wash the smell off my hands and breath (so my mom wouldn't discover what I was up to) was a real challenge.

The teens would buy a smoke from some older kid who'd stole them from their parents or talked another adult into buying them a whole pack.

Lunch money became habit-supporting funds. By the time I was a senior in high school, I was a full-on smoker. I didn't think much about it until I had to pass my military physical fitness test, which involved a lot of running. By that time, I was up to a pack a day before I started wondering why I smoked.

I wasn't a typical smoker. As I mentioned earlier, it was a love/hate relationship. I was obsessive compulsive about not smoking in my house or car. After every smoke, I'd wash my hands and pop a mint in my mouth. I didn't want to smell like a smoker. I would quit for a while, using nicotine patches, hypnosis, and quitting cold turkey.

My longest stint as a non-smoker was ten years . . . ten years and a traumatic family event landed me right back to them. Was it a coping mechanism? I'm guessing it was, but for what reason I had no clue. Something about smoking held the stress of life and the past at bay.

Many years later, I was ready to give quitting another try. I made an appointment with an NLP (Neurolinguistic Programming) practitioner to help me stop smoking for good. NLP is basically using eye movement and language to reprogram how the brain sorts and deals with various stressors, trauma, etc.

After arriving for my appointment, the practitioner explained what she'd be doing and how I would assist in reprogramming my own neural pathways linked to smoking. She had me sit in a comfortable chair and follow her finger with my eyes as she said various things.

We weren't very far into the hour-long appointment when (after one of the eye movements) I began sobbing uncontrollably! She was doing her best to reassure me and put me at ease, but I wasn't able to do anything about what was happening. Suddenly I stood up, arms at my side, palms out, and began saying something over and over again in a different language. I didn't know this language, but it felt like I was saying some sort of prayer. I was aware of what I was doing, but had no control over it happening. I then started turning counterclockwise while continuing the "prayer".

My practitioner had to step out of the room while I continued to cry my eyes out and repeat foreign words over and over again. Not sure how long this event lasted (2-3 minutes?), but I did stop crying and speaking in another tongue.

The lady came back into the room and asked me how I was doing. I felt physically and emotionally drained. I apologized for what had happened and for scaring her. She seemed to understand, but didn't feel we should continue with the session that day. I totally understood. So, after I'd rested in my car for a few minutes and calmed down enough to drive, I headed home. I was so tired by the time I made the 45-minute drive home that I went straight to bed and slept for hours.

I never scheduled a follow-up session. Partly because I was afraid something might happen again. Partly because I was embarrassed and couldn't stand the thought of facing my NLP practitioner again. I attempted to make sense of what had happened that day. It seemed I had kept stuff bottled up inside me for so long that it chose that very moment to be released. After all the things I'd been through in life (like the ones mentioned in my memoir) without an outlet, it wasn't surprising that a ton of it just spewed out like a geyser.

Not that I had any clue this would be the moment. No forewarning . . . no feeling anything coming on . . . nothing.

So, I continued to be a smoker for a few more years, quitting here and there without lasting results. All up until the day I'd had enough and was truly ready to quit for good. The day I was done.

But that's a story for another time.

4
Murdered in Mena

On Tuesday, April 25, 2017, a woman's body was found face-down in a creek in the shadow of the Ouachita Mountains (Wah-Che-Tah). The following day, an employer called the Sheriff's Office to report one of their employees had not showed up for work all week. Police did a welfare check at the employee's home, but did not locate the employee. They did find a 37-year-old man at the home and arrested him on an outstanding warrant.

The call to law enforcement by the employer, and the subsequent welfare check by local police, would be the catalyst for an all-out, four-day, intensive search by over 70 members of local, state, and federal agencies. Not only was the employee still missing, but also her two children (aged two and nine). That evening, authorities issued a Morgan Nick Amber Alert for the children and listed them as missing and endangered.

Working the day shift at the State Capitol Complex, I overheard colleagues talking about a mom and her two kids missing from their home in Mena, Arkansas. As word spread, many employees began connecting their computers and phones to news channels for updates. Local law enforcement had deployed every kind of search resource available to them, but by nightfall there was still no trace of the missing children or their mother.

The next morning, everyone at work was again monitoring TV and the Internet for any updates. Law enforcement had intensified their search efforts. The developing story seemed to be on every news and radio station, saturating social media, and the talk of everyone in the state.

On my lunch break, I decided to eat in my car and grab a few minutes of relaxation. My thoughts drifted back to the mom and children police were desperately searching for. As each hour ticked by, everyone knew the odds of finding them alive were quickly dissipating. The thought was in the back of everyone's minds, but nobody dared speak it. A mixed feeling of hope and dread hung thick in the air.

As I'm sitting in my car trying to relax, I hear "too late" in a young boy's voice. In that moment, I knew it was the voice of the missing nine-year-old boy. "Oh, my God!"

A sudden wave of tears and grief hit me like a brick. My chest began to tighten (I felt his heart hurting). I knew the boy was telling me they were **ALL** already dead!

Thursday brought a double dose of tragic news to the unfolding story. The woman found in the creek was positively identified as the missing employee AND mother of the two missing children! When law enforcement went to deliver the death notification to the victim's next of kin, they discovered yet another body. The deceased was that of the children's great-uncle.

After this gruesome discovery, finding the children became even more critical for searchers. (Even though I knew none of them would be found alive, I couldn't say anything. It would have been viewed as awkward, or downright mean.)

Authorities ramped up their search to an insane level, desperately searching for the two-year-old little girl and her nine-year-old brother. News coverage of their courageous, unrelenting search (and photos of the children) filled local, national, and international newspapers. The top story (and every "breaking news" or "special report" of the day) was about the search for these poor children. Many Arkansans held their breath and prayed for the safe return of these innocents.

All hope was pretty much lost on Friday. The news came that authorities had found the little girl's body. They found her not far from the creek where her mother had been discovered. The devastating news could be seen on the weary faces of the law enforcement professionals who had the unenviable task of holding the press conference that day. After delivering the sad news, they called for renewed efforts to locate the brother of the two-year-old. Searchers still held out hope he would be found alive. Then came Saturday . . .

As the all-out search for the brother continued into Saturday, Arkansas State Police interviewed the 37-year-old man they had arrested on an outstanding warrant at the employee's home on April 26. During that interview, the man told investigators he had killed ALL FOUR family members and offered to show them where the body of the boy (the one who had whispered to me) was located. So, the state police drove to the area the man directed them to, where they found the last body.

On Monday, May 1st (seven days after the mother was discovered in the creek), the man arrested at her home was charged with four counts of capital murder in the deaths of the mother, her two children, and her uncle.

It seemed everyone across the state was sad and bewildered by all that had happened over the three or so days of the search. Collectively, we shed many a tear, said many a prayer, and in the end none could be saved.

5
Dental Delirium

Not all of my paranormal moments are tragic. Some involve normal routines that suddenly take an insane turn and go off the rails with no warning. One of those times involved a routine visit with my dentist.

I'd been experiencing some pain and sensitivity in a tooth for about a week, so I contacted my dentist and scheduled an appointment. Two days later I arrived for my appointment, checked in, then had a seat in the waiting area. My dentist's office is bright and comfortable, and always has a good vibe to it. After selecting a magazine from one of the tables and skimming through its contents, my name was called and I was escorted back to one of the treatment rooms.

Like many other people, visiting the dentist isn't exactly on my list of favorite things to do. Having experienced a couple of very painful procedures in the past doesn't help boost my personal ranking of dental care either.

Even though it's been years since my last painful event, I think somewhere, in the back of my mind, the dread from past experiences creeps in. The other things that help make dental care a least liked activity (for me) are the cost and the inability to get the problem solved in one visit.

The dental assistant seated me in the exam chair and started prepping me (and the instruments) for the dentist. My dentist is wonderful and it had been a long time since my last difficult procedure. I wasn't worried about anything going wrong with a simple exam. My dentist came in, asked me questions, and poked around in my mouth, focusing on the area that was causing pain. After an X-ray, she informed me that my tooth was infected and I'd have to take an antibiotic for the next week. After that, I'd come back and have the tooth extracted.

No problem. I had my prescription filled at the pharmacy and took my first dose. A little while later, I wasn't feeling very well and decided to get some sleep.

The next day (still not feeling well), I took another dose of the antibiotic. Within an hour or so, my throat started swelling and I could hardly speak! Something was wrong. I called the dentist and was told to stop taking the medication (apparently, I was allergic to that particular type of antibiotic). They prescribed a different antibiotic for me to finish out my week-long treatment.

After a week, my infection was under control and I returned to the dentist to have my tooth pulled. I had no worries about the procedure as I'd had a tooth extracted in the past. My dentist came in, explained the process, numbed the area (with the big needle I dislike greatly), and started her work. Everything was going smoothly. Concern was furthest from my mind. I'd never had a bad experience in her treatment room. She carefully removed the tooth without too much of a struggle.

Then it happened . . .

From out of nowhere, this rush of grief overtook me and I began sobbing uncontrollably! It caught me off guard. I had no idea what I was crying about, but I couldn't stop it either! Not only was I crying, but I was wailing as well! My dentist thought she had done something to me to cause this reaction. She asked me if I was okay. I found that I couldn't speak!

All I could do was shake my head "No". Then I couldn't breathe! My dentist asked me what was wrong, but I couldn't speak. I noticed other people peeking into the room out of concern.

The dental assistant and my dentist both were directing me to take deep breaths and relax. They were trying to get me to stop the loud sobs at least. More questions came. Are you okay? Is there anyone we can call? I was crying and sobbing like someone had just notified me of a death in the family or something! I was also scared because I was just there, witnessing all this, not able to stop it.

After a few minutes of deep breathing (as best I could), I began to relax. The body-shuddering sobs and wailing stopped. My tears dried up. I sat there looking at the people in the room, concern still on their faces. Finally able to speak, I told them I was okay. My dentist seemed to think I had a panic or anxiety attack. That wasn't what happened, but I agreed with her to make everyone else feel better and have an answer as to why this weirdness happened. I'd never had an anxiety or panic attack in my entire life!

After I was calm and back in the "here and now", I walked out of the treatment room to side glances from other employees and their patients. The lady who took my payment seemed concerned about me. I assured her that I was okay. Making my way through the waiting room (and out the front door) couldn't happen fast enough! Once outside, I breathed a sigh of relief, but was still bewildered by what had just taken place. I still wasn't used to the random outbursts that set upon me when I least expected them (and in awkward situations).

Looking back on the whole drama, it seems pulling the tooth was the catalyst for a spontaneous releasing of anger, frustration, trauma, pain, and a host of other emotions that I'd been carrying around for a very long time. I felt bad for the staff, but I had no way to control when, where, or what might trigger these types of releases.

I've not returned to that dentist's office since.

6
No Good Will Come of This

We never know how things are going to turn out, but now and then we see a glimpse into the future and hope it doesn't come true. Sometimes we can hope, pray, and bargain . . . all to no avail. An insight I received about a future event didn't show itself for years, but I could feel it hanging around . . . waiting.

Would this premonition reveal itself as quickly as an eagle catches a lake trout . . . unseen until the moment it strikes without warning? Would it fail to come to pass because of a choice to walk a different path? The hope was for a change in direction that would make the "squatter" hanging around me vanish without consequence. However, the way life played out, the eagle came instead.

The toddler had so much energy and a desire to explore his world. His eyes were deep . . . as if they could look into your soul. When he smiled, it made people happy. He was a cute boy who had it bad growing up. Way worse than many have lived through. He just wanted to be loved, to explore, and have fun (like most children). He didn't receive any of those things. Maybe in short-lived, small doses that left him wondering when (or if) he would ever be lucky enough to get another taste.

Walking on eggshells and staying small were games he learned to play very early in life. They were the only strategies he had to avoid his mother's wrath. Some of the time they worked, but at times, no matter how small he made himself (or how quiet he stayed), explosive anger still found him. He was the punching bag for a woman who had a hair-trigger temper and no off switch. At any point in time, one could see various injuries in different stages of healing.

Neighbors, family members, and complete strangers would periodically call CPS (Child Protective Services) out of concern for the young boy. Even though the home was visited multiple times by law enforcement and CPS over the years, nothing changed for the boy. At some point, the harassment from the authorities became too much for the mother.

Her strategy was to make a "fresh start" in another town where CPS and police didn't know her history. By this time, the mother had three children she was regularly abusing.

The fresh start didn't last long. Her new neighbors started reporting the abuse and neglect they witnessed. For a moment, it seemed the years of calls and visits about the abuse would finally result in action to help the children. But, just as hope had risen, the mother vanished along with her three kids.

It was like they simply disappeared. The mother hadn't told anyone about moving. Her apartment wasn't cleaned out. Relatives searched for them, but they were nowhere to be found. The family was concerned for the safety of the children. A state of shock, mixed with fear and helplessness, set in. Heads filled with scary thoughts.

Had their mom been kidnapped or killed? Did she move in with some guy in another town? Were the children being sold or trafficked? Were they all dead, buried some place where they'd never be found? There were many questions, but no answers. No answers for a long time.

Ten years passed before the eagle, waiting on the fringes of my subconscious, came swooping in. The fast dive it chose (taking mere seconds) struck with pinpoint accuracy, and left total devastation in its wake. No one saw the eagle coming . . . and no one would soon forget the day it came. The little boy (who had endured so much throughout his life) was now a teenager sitting in jail . . . charged with two counts of capital murder.

A few months after another call to CPS went nowhere, I graduated from high school and left the toxic environment I had been living in for over two years. On the day I left, I gave that little boy a hug, told him I loved him, and said goodbye. I felt compelled to look at him one last time before I got into the car to leave. As I did, I felt time slow down and heard, "No good will come of this." It made me sad, but also frustrated because I wasn't able to help him get out of his abusive environment.

It was about three years later when I received word that his mother had vanished, seemingly into thin air. Another eight years passed before I learned a relative had known their whereabouts from the beginning. It was like being an unwilling participant in some crazy-ass TV reality show! I felt happy because at least they were still alive. For years, doubt concerning their well-being hung like a black cloud over life.

An additional two years or so went by before I received a phone call that changed everything. That phone call told me where the kids had ended up after they had "vanished" with their mother.

This news came so far from left field that I had trouble grasping it. It was like my brain couldn't process the information. My knees went weak, and I felt like someone had punched me in the stomach really hard.

The slow-motion vision and message I'd heard (when he was a child) came back to me. The scene played repeatedly in my mind. I couldn't wrap my head around the enormity of it all. I cried for days and tried grasping onto some little straw of reality. Surely, this could not be!

The now teenaged boy had committed a crime so heinous that an entire city (and possibly a whole state) was ready for a public hanging. The crime scene photos were ghastly. It was obvious the paramedics tried desperately to save one victim. Such heroic actions weren't necessary for the second victim, who died instantly.

My tears flowed for those poor souls who were just going about their daily life. They had no warning of the chaos, fear, and suffering that awaited them when they woke up that day.

For me, I felt like I was in the middle of some horrible nightmare. None of it seemed real. I asked God, "Please, wake me up! Please!" but I WAS awake.

Testifying on his behalf was one of the hardest things I've ever done. The hope was that once the jury heard the stories of his long-term abuse and neglect, they would decide to spare him the death penalty. Being smack-dab in the middle of a state that's proud of their death penalty (and carries out said punishment on the regular), the odds of swaying the jury were slim.

But letting everyone know what he had endured his entire life at the hands of his mother needed to be made public. Perhaps she would have to answer to the justice system when all was said and done. It was beyond sad that the boy never really had a chance at a decent life.

After testifying, I left the courtroom and found a place to sit. As I sat down, I just spontaneously exploded into body-shuddering sobs I could not control. My face was wet, snot was pouring from my nose, and I was wailing to the heavens. All the events of the last twenty years reared their ugly heads. All the pain, sorrow, failure, loss, and helplessness rode on those tears. I was inconsolable. Passers-by took a wide berth. It was the third time in my life I felt like I would lose my mind.

When the trials ended, he was convicted of two counts of capital murder. His sentence was death by lethal injection. Tears of grief and relief filled the courtroom. Although the horrible story of what the child went through in his brief life was told by relatives, schools, CPS from two states, and doctors, they were unsuccessful in having his life spared.

After the first trial concluded, I visited the teenager in the county jail. I hadn't seen him in about thirteen years. He looked like a grown man! We talked through a thick, plexiglass-type cell. I told him I loved him. He was happy to see me! He still had those deep eyes and a catching smile . . . although a sad one. He seemed happy and grateful that I tried, once again, to save him.

As his execution date neared (after years of appeals), I wanted to do something to help him during that process. I was worried that maybe his fear of death, or the weight of what he had done, might somehow interrupt his smooth transition. In other words, I was concerned for his soul after all that had happened. He chose not to have any witnesses at his execution. So, I decided to perform a ceremony for him that ensured his spirit went where it was supposed to go quickly, with no time for hesitation or distraction.

The ceremony involved four days of no food, prayer, and envisioning him going into The Light. Regardless of what people believe about God, I'd like to think we all want people to go where they're supposed to go when they die. (Personally, I don't want spirits hanging out where they're not supposed to be.) So, I fasted, prayed, and dreamt . . . over and over. For four days I sent him the love I felt for him . . . the love he never received in this life. I shared my good memories of him and told him all the things he had taught me. I also let him know that everything would be alright and that there was no need to be scared.

The day of his execution arrived. I didn't know what time it would happen. Still within my Sacred Circle, I called the horses to give him a swift ride to the Other Side. After the call, I drifted in and out of consciousness for a while. Suddenly, I felt a deep sense of peace unlike any I'd ever known. I looked up at the clock and noted the time. He was gone, and I knew it . . . felt it in my bones. And just like that, the little boy with deep eyes and an infectious smile was no more. My mourning for him started in that moment.

After a while, I picked myself up off the floor, gave thanks, and closed my circle. I thought long about what had just transpired.

God and the angels let me know he was safely on the Other Side. My duty was done. I no longer had to worry about him, pray for him, or fight for him. The divine help I received that day was a reminder that God does indeed answer prayers. For all of it, I felt truly blessed.

Sometime later, I logged onto the Department of Corrections website for news on death sentences carried out that day. I found and read the story about his execution. The reporter listed the time they pronounced him dead. It was the exact time I had noted when the feeling of peace came over me. Some people don't believe things like this can happen. I experienced it, so I know it DOES happen and IS possible.

Years later (after his execution), the boy's spirit came and shared with me the truth about what he did on that horrible day. He knew there was one detail I just couldn't wrap my head around. One I didn't want to believe (or wasn't capable of believing). He told me it happened just the way the prosecutor said it did. He also told me why he did it. Even after death, he didn't want me having any unanswered questions. He wanted me to be at peace with everything.

7
Slo-Mo 18-Wheeler

Most of the cases that catch my attention result in a one-off, or a single psychic event/experience related to them. The most bizarre serial killer case of the 20th and 21st centuries would take me down a rabbit hole leading to multiple strange and unusual moments over the years. This particular case was the catalyst for a phenomenon I hadn't yet experienced in all my previous psychic events: what I chose to call a "psychic alarm". This is how it all started . . .

The case was that of The Long Island Serial Killer, or LISK (also referred to as The Gilgo Beach Killer and The Craigslist Ripper.) This case caught my attention almost from the start. I had watched *The Killing Season* (an eight-part, 2016 documentary about the crimes, the victims, and the sketchy behavior by the lead law enforcement agency).

The two documentary investigators (Joshua Zeman and Rachel Mills) began the series in New York, then uncovered information that took them to Atlantic City, NJ; Daytona Beach, FL; Albuquerque, NM; Charleston, WV; then back to New York, NY. They started to think that maybe the LISK travels to other areas to commit his crimes.

During their investigation in Daytona Beach, they interviewed an author, a reporter, and a private investigator. These professionals had pieced together a puzzle of once seemingly unrelated missing women in their area. As they continued digging deeper, and broadening their scope, they discovered more women, all last seen (or their bodies discovered) along Florida's highways. At some point they realized that missing and deceased women connected to the Interstate highway system weren't just a Florida problem . . . but a nationwide one.

Zeman and Mills then learned of the FBI's Highway Serial Killings Initiative (HSK). HSK is a "specialized program that addresses a pattern of unsolved murders where victims, often vulnerable women such as sex workers, hitchhikers, or runaways, are picked up in one jurisdiction, murdered in another, and dumped along highways in a third, making jurisdictional cooperation difficult" (FBI.gov website).

The author, reporter, and private investigator in Florida were on to this phenomenon even before the FBI announced their initiative.

An analyst from the Oklahoma State Bureau of Investigation identified (in 2004) a recurring pattern of bodies found along Interstate 40 in Oklahoma, Arkansas, Mississippi, and Texas. Her findings were the origin of the FBI's initiative, which helps local law enforcement agencies connect these types of cases across different states.

"The FBI suspects that long-haul truckers are ideal perpetrators for these crimes due to their mobility, which allows them to operate across multiple jurisdictions, and the isolation of their work environment, which provides opportunities for victim selection and anonymous body disposal. The initiative's database, which began with around 500 victims and 200 potential suspects, now includes at least 850 homicides linked to long-haul truck drivers over the past few decades. As of 2024, there were approximately 450 suspects under investigation, with 25 truckers already in prison for multiple murders" (FBI.gov website).

Needless to say, I was blown away by the sheer number of victims AND serial killers!

After learning about the Highway Serial Killings Initiative, the documentarians interviewed a convicted long-haul trucker serial killer. He told them how he would pick up the women, keep them captive in the sleeper, kill them, then dispose of their bodies. What came next was a twist that made the whole already horrific details even more ghastly. The killer talked about a network of truckers who would exchange or share their victims with members of their group. He spoke of it in a matter-of-fact way, describing how they knew the other truckers' "preferences", and would meet with them at truck stops to make "swaps" or "gifts". Listening to the serial killer talk about their murderous group behavior made me realize normal people have no idea what's out there in our world.

A few months later, I decided to go on a road trip through a section of the Ozark National Forest. Scenic 7 Byway is a great choice to have a beautiful, relaxing drive or enjoy other activities like hiking, horseback riding, canoeing, or mountain biking. The Byway runs from Missouri to Louisiana for 290 miles (467 km) and has a variety of topography and scenic vistas to enjoy. The forest is also home to over 500 species of trees and woody plants. After spending most of the day taking in nature's scents and beauty, I pulled into a truck stop for a much-needed bathroom break, bite to eat, and fueling up the car.

SLO-MO 18-WHEELER

The truck stop was surrounded by the remnants of the forest I'd just visited. I decided to sit outside for a few minutes while enjoying the sandwich I'd purchased. After finishing my snack, I deposited my trash into the bin and started making my way toward my car. I hadn't made it very far across the huge parking lot when I noticed a big rig (18-wheeler) approaching, headed toward the exit. I stopped to wait for the truck to pass before continuing to my car.

As I looked up to watch the truck go by, I felt time slowing down! My whole body stiffened as a chill went all the way up my spine. My mind was screaming, "Danger! Danger!" Everything went quiet. Not a sound from the truck, other people visiting the store, or even the birds! Everything I saw and felt in that moment was stuck in this place of silence where time was moving at half-speed. I turned my head ever so slowly from left to right to watch the truck pass by. As the cab of the truck passed my line of sight, the hair on the back of my neck stood up in a full scalp crawl! The window of the sleeper compartment was covered. At that moment I knew the driver had someone in the back of that truck that didn't want to be there!

After the truck had cleared the roadway, time went back to normal. The sounds of people, birds, and cars could be heard again. An overwhelming urge to stop the truck and search it, or call the police and have them search it, came over me. The compelling feeling was screaming at me! After a moment or two, reality sank in. I had no authority to pull the truck over and no reason to call the police (one they would take seriously).

My mind quickly switched to working on an alternate plan . . . call the police and lie. Tell them I heard screams coming from the truck as it passed. But in those moments of being overwhelmed by the experience, I didn't get the license plate number or the make of the truck. The only information I could have provided to police was a white male driving a gold-tone truck with capped sleeper windows.

Sometimes I wonder who the person was in that sleeper compartment. Some might argue that I really didn't **know** someone was being held against their will in that truck. My response would be, I KNOW there was someone in that truck that didn't want to be there. It was like I became a human tracking system and the signal originated from that truck! My memory about what transpired that day has never changed. I know what I know.

One of the things I couldn't understand about the whole event was the complete silence. It was literally like someone (or something) had shut off my hearing or turned off the world's audio! Maybe it was for my protection. Perhaps I wasn't supposed to hear the noises coming from the truck. It's possible the silence served as an attention getter . . . forcing me to pay attention. Either way, this type of visceral experience hasn't repeated itself (yet) since that day.

Next time I'll be better prepared.

8

Missing Kentucky Mom

On the evening of January 4, 2019, a young mother of four decided to go out on the town. Having just given birth to twins, it had been a while since she had been out with friends. She and a friend headed out to the city around 9 p.m. to blow off some steam and have fun. They stopped by a friend's house and had a couple of drinks before he drove the two women to a local bar in town. A couple of hours later, the male friend left because he had to be up early the next morning. Within a short time, the other friend wanted to go home, but the mom wanted to stay until the bar closed down. Apparently, this caused an argument between them, so her other friend ended up leaving the bar as well.

Now, at the bar alone, the mom met a group of men and at some point agreed to continue the party at one of their houses.

They said they'd give her a ride home whenever she was ready. On the way to their house, the mom called her own mother on FaceTime at around 3 a.m. and told her she was fine and would be back home later that morning. The mother didn't detect anything wrong and her daughter seemed happy, so she was reassured, and the call ended.

When daylight came, there was no sign of the mom or the car she'd been driving. She didn't return home later that morning. By that evening, panic had set in with her family. Her mother filed a missing persons report and reported the car she had been driving as stolen. Her family was left wondering where she was. They knew she would never leave her kids. Friends started looking for her and passing out flyers. Her car was later found abandoned in a neighborhood, but there was no sign of the missing mom. Police allowed the mother to come and pick up the car as it didn't hold any clues to her disappearance.

Not long after the missing persons search started, police released images of the mom with two men (one black and one Caucasian) that had been captured on surveillance cameras. They asked the public for help in identifying the men and locating the mom. It didn't take long for the investigators to figure out there were three men who left with her, and brought them in for questioning.

In the months that followed, investigators conducted aerial searches, searched a landfill and nearby burn piles, and sorted through thousands of tips. They also conducted multiple interviews in an attempt to find the young mom.

All their efforts weren't resulting in a break in the case. The search area was pretty large due to the distances the mom had traveled that evening. Multiple counties and cities were in the search area. The search and investigation continued to drag on for a little over six months. Then came the tip . . . A relative of the Caucasian man in the photo would end the difficult search for the mom. The relative had been digging in a strawberry patch on the family farm when he uncovered something that had a strong odor. Law enforcement was notified.

When the investigators arrived at the relative's house, they uncovered the mom's body in a 19"-deep grave. She had been wrapped in plastic trash bags, her body folded over with a rug behind her back. Her body was unclothed and her feet bound with tape.

A previous search of the home of the Caucasian male found blood connected to the mom on a closet door inside his bedroom.

When her remains were located, the rug found there was believed to have been taken from his room. According to police testimony, the day after the mom's disappearance, the male had reached out to a family member to ask where she'd bought the rug that had been in his room, and said he planned to buy another one.

Later that day he bought the rug, and it was in his room when police searched the home five days after the young mom went missing. In the same search of his home, an investigator's report noted that the house looked like it had recently been cleaned. Multiple walls looked like the bottom half had been wiped down. The report also said that what appeared to be blood spatter was found on some of the walls, including inside the man's bedroom closet.

One question that was never answered publicly was the cause of death. The amount of time her body was buried destroyed any evidence for medical examiners to use to determine cause of death. The Caucasian male pleaded guilty to murdering the mom, but didn't provide any details of how he killed her in his confession. The mom's best friend, and the godmother of her children, said she still had some questions. "The whole story is still a mystery and I don't think, until he comes forward at one point in his life and tells us the story, we will ever know."

The day law enforcement released images of the mom and men, I happened to catch the breaking news update. As soon as they showed the photos I said aloud, "Oh, she's dead." I didn't hear anything or see anything . . . I just <u>knew</u> it . . . instantly. After that happened, I took a look at each man in the image and was drawn to the Caucasian male. I felt he was the killer. When looking at his image, it stood out from the others, almost like he was highlighted. Also, something about him felt "off", like a negative vibe that emanated from him. Information about any other possible suspects didn't come to me.

While this story was unfolding, I was in the middle of completing a psychic detective course. The class was at the point in the course where our instructor gave us an active case to practice the skills we had learned. The only details we were given were that it was a recent missing persons case of a woman in the U.S. Our assignment was to practice the method of obtaining clues we had been taught in class. Using that method, I described a woman, dirty blond hair (real color brown), partially covered by brush/limbs in wet soil (like in a damp area that would be near a body of water). A smell of dampness filled my nostrils. I also noticed a water tower with a cell tower close by.

Based on the information I received during my practice (and had shared with my class), my instructor asked me to forward it to her. Later I discovered the case we had been practicing with was that of the "Kentucky Mom". After the case was solved, I went back and looked at all the information I had psychically received. The Caucasian male from the image police shared in the media had indeed murdered the young mom (he confessed). Her hair was naturally brown, but dyed blond. She was killed at a house that had a view of a water tower. There wasn't a lake by where she was found, but there were many ponds in the area where she was buried.

In a bizarre twist of coincidence, I discovered the main road connecting the street where the killer's house sat bore the same name as the city the mom was living in prior to her disappearance!

9
Death From the Inside Out

Older sisters are the cool siblings. We look up to them while growing up. They seem so much older and wiser. If we're lucky, we get to hang out with them as we mature. Maybe get into a little harmless trouble while searching for something fun to do. Share secrets with each other when we're getting along. Betray every secret when we're in trouble or not getting along. Have each other's backs when fights break out. Often, we believe this sisterly bond will withstand the test of time. In our naivety, we forget that we never know what the future may bring.

Childhood memories of my elder sister are few. Partially because of the time that has passed since our growing-up years.

Most likely because she was five years older than me. We didn't have the same friends or go to the same schools for long. From my point of view, my sister was always sad. Maybe our home life (along with the racism, bullying, and school fights) made her sad. If I were to guess, I'd say all my siblings were sad kids. When you're young, you don't notice how sad you are, but you can see the sadness on the faces and in the eyes of other people. I clearly remember that, like me, my sister loved spending time on my grandparents' farm.

We all worked hard on the farm, but it made us feel alive and gave us a sense of belonging. It kept the family working together, food on the table, and ensured there was enough firewood to make it through the winter. One blessing from spending time on the farm was that the hassles of inner-city and home-life drama disappeared. The farm was the only place where we got a breather from the chaos and abuse in our lives. We all seemed a lot happier there. Given the choice, we would have lived there forever (at least I would have). Sadly, our life stories weren't written that way.

My sister and I grew up with the same dad until my mom divorced him when I was in elementary school. My elder sister had different physical features and a different last name than the rest of us.

As kids, we didn't notice stuff like that. We were all just brothers and sisters.

In her early teens, my sister was told a family secret about her biological dad. One of our aunts revealed who her real dad was and what had happened between him and our mom. Her life, and ours, would change dramatically after that.

It wasn't long after the big secret was out in the open that my sister started acting differently. She was constantly getting into trouble and running away. Her behavior got so bad she was sent to a juvenile facility for a time. When she came back home she was different somehow. The juvenile home didn't seem to have helped her much. One could say she was worse off instead of "rehabilitated". Maybe she suffered abuse while she was there (like so many youths we hear about on the news or social media). What really happened there? No one can say for sure. I don't remember her ever talking about it. I know life didn't improve for her, me, or my baby sister after that.

Not long after my sister returned home, my mom found a man she wanted to marry. She had been divorced for a few years and felt she was ready for another relationship. Her fiancé became the reason we felt afraid to go to sleep at night.

We didn't understand what was happening at first. He would sneak into our rooms after everyone was asleep. We would wake up and he'd be standing in our room . . . staring at us. We were terrified every night we would wake up with a hand fondling our private parts. He'd leave the room quickly if we woke up.

For a while, each of us thought we were the only one experiencing the nightly stalking. One day (out of the blue), my elder sister and I started talking about the night creeper we had in common. I don't remember what sparked the conversation. Then we decided to ask our younger sister if she had been keeping the same secret. She had. I guess we had kept this awful secret to ourselves because of the feelings we didn't know what to do with. A sense of relief washed over us once we knew we shared the same secret.

We were afraid to tell our mom about our abuser, but even more afraid of what could happen if we kept it a secret. We stuck together (like *The Three Musketeers*) and told our mom what had been going on while she slept. As you can imagine, all hell broke loose after our sit-down with our mom. She kicked his sorry ass to the curb that very day!

Our lives had changed forever (although we didn't know it at the time), but we solved that HUGE problem together with courage and strength! After feeling weak and helpless for so long, we felt empowered!

I was proud of my sisters that day (and still am). It's sad to say, but this was also the time I felt closest to my elder sister. Strange how things get categorized in our minds. That powerful time is how I choose to remember my elder sister.

Once we got through the drama with our mom's fiancé, I didn't see my sister much. It's like she faded from my memory somehow. At some point, she ran away again and never came back. Years passed before we reconnected again through a series of events that had left me homeless. Moving in with my elder sister was the only solution I had at the time, except foster care. My new life became full-time student, babysitter, and housekeeper. It wasn't long before the full weight of how much my sister had changed became apparent to me. This arrangement became one of the most trying periods of my life.

My once positive (but sad) memories of my sister were almost immediately shattered. She had become a verbally and physically abusive person with a hair-trigger temper.

Her wrath was taken out on whoever was unlucky enough to be in close proximity. The negative in my life was cascading out of control. All I wanted to do was graduate high school and leave that place forever.

After two years or so, I managed to graduate high school despite the chaos and misery. Within a short time, I had joined the military and left that horrible place and situation. A few years later, my sister would disappear with her three children. The next time I laid eyes on my sister was about ten years later during a week-long penalty phase of a criminal trial. She refused to look at, or talk to, me. She wouldn't allow me to come into her house to talk with my niece. I had to visit with my niece in my car.

Another fifteen years would pass before another chapter about my sister would be written. She had worked at a meat-processing plant for years. One day she was a no-show for her shift. After waiting some time for my sister to show up, a co-worker decided to drive to her house and check on her. The co-worker found my sister unresponsive in her home and called for an ambulance. She was rushed to the hospital and underwent a barrage of tests to try and figure out what had happened.

After all the tests had come back, the doctors diagnosed her with end-stage cancer. Reconciling the past between us was my hope, but when I asked to visit her, she refused. All I could do was pray for her healing and the healing of our past.

The specialists determined her cancer had progressed beyond any available treatment. There was nothing more they could do except offer hospice care. My sister died about two months after her diagnosis.

I had traveled to a conference (and was just about to start my work day) when I got the news. Just like when I was notified of my brother's death, I wasn't able to stand. My tears kept flowing for a while. A co-worker made sure I got home. On the drive back, I kept thinking about it being too late. Too late to bridge the divide between us. Too late to really listen to each other. Too late to say the words that needed to be said.

My hope was to attend her funeral and start the grieving process, but my sister had made it clear to her family that I was not welcome at her funeral service. There would be no reconciliation or healing . . . or so I thought.

Just a few days after my sister's death, I had an appointment with a medium. The session had been scheduled a week or so before my sister passed. I decided to keep the appointment. What could it hurt at this point? The medium showed me to her room and had me take a seat. After explaining her process, the session began and my sister showed up immediately!

She told me she understood why I did what I did so many years ago. She also apologized for being so bull-headed. Her telling me there was nothing I could have done to save my nephew's life gave me relief. She also said everything was now in divine order and not to blame myself. Then she told me she loved me and the medium started hearing the song *We Are Family* by Sister Sledge.

After receiving all that information during the mediumship session, it took a few days to process it in my mind. The things my sister had said really helped me start grieving her loss. After about a week of being a total wreck from releasing a range of emotions and tears, I finally felt almost normal. There was a part of me that was missing, but I could make it through my daily routine again. It felt like I had released the majority of all those years of drama and trauma. Life was getting better again. I felt in control and stronger. Silly rabbit . . .

A few weeks after my sister died, I woke up, had coffee, took a shower, and got ready for work. Everything seemed normal as I headed out to my car and started my daily commute. About halfway into my drive, the song *Photograph* by Nickelback started playing on the radio. Hearing the lyrics, "Look at this photograph. Every time I do it makes me laugh . . .", a sudden wave of grief hit me and I burst into tears!

It came with such abruptness that I had to quickly pull off the road into a parking lot. I had a spontaneous grieving session for my sister that lasted about ten to fifteen minutes!

Maybe the lyrics to that song didn't mean what I was making them about. I believe my sister sent the song to me because she was sad about how things were between us in the end. Maybe she wanted us to reminisce about the happier times we had together when we were young. I don't pretend to know all the stuff my sister went through.

It seems she never got over the secret revealed to her when she was a teenager. Maybe it made her question the whole concept of who she was, what she believed, and her trust in others. Perhaps it's why she started running away and other things.

When I see her again, I'll ask her about this stuff, but until then I'd only be guessing. Right now we're cool, and stuff has worked itself out, so I'm good with it.

10
The Flashing Red Number 3

We've all had those times in our life when the phone rings late at night, or early in the morning before sunrise, and you know something must be wrong. Sometimes it's a wrong number or a teenager who stayed out way past curfew and needs a ride home. Other times it's one of those friends or family members that trouble seems to follow, and the late calls are from a nearby jail or police station.

When my phone rang it was early evening and the voice on the other end was familiar. I assumed it was to catch up on what had been going on in our lives since the last time we'd talked. It wasn't. It was to let me know about someone who was gravely ill.

Her chances of recovery were slim to none. So much so that she'd been placed in in-home hospice care.

The familiar voice on the other end was aware of my psychic abilities and asked me if I was "getting anything". When I asked, I immediately saw a flashing red number three. That was it. No other information. So, I told the caller what I was seeing, and he asked me what I thought it meant. I replied that it felt like a measure of time, and since the number was red AND flashing, it meant urgency (time was short). "What does that mean?" he asked. "Three years, three months, or three days?" Understandably, he needed clarification. The time didn't feel like years or days (but I wasn't receiving any more specifics), so I told him what sort of time it was feeling like to me.

I asked if there was anything I could do to help. He said there was and that he would call me and let me know. He sounded overwhelmed from all he had going on. We ended our call and I sat there and cried. I cried for his loved one and for him. Theirs was a story of finding happiness after a long and disheartening search, only for it to be cut short before it even started.

A few days passed and I didn't get another call letting me know what I could do to help. After another day or two, I woke up in the morning and felt this urgent (emergent) need to pack my car and go. I kept hearing, "Time to leave! Time to leave!" over and over again.

I talked to my landlady about having a family emergency and needing to leave. She was nice about my sudden move. I started donating and/or selling just about everything I owned.

A winter storm was headed our way, with a second one forecasted for a few days later. The window for my safe departure was closing fast. Living in a colder climate, the weather forecasts are an important consideration for traveling by air or automobile. The trick is to time your departure at the best possible break in the bad weather. I did just that, and the best time to hightail it out of there was the coming weekend.

I was living my life in overdrive, taking care of all my loose ends, checking my car over, and packing it like a sardine can for the thousand or so mile trip. The first storm passed and I made a break for the open highway. It had been a little over a week after I received that first phone call.

I said a prayer for a safe and quick drive across the country. The drive went by fast with the miles becoming one big blur. Driving through Kansas was boring, but I drove like a bat out of hell, blasting Native American Pow-wow music to stay awake. Too many times to remember pushing the auto scan, trying to find a radio station that wouldn't put me to sleep or preach at me for being a sinner.

Having to use the bathroom so bad, I stuffed a handful of napkins down my pants just in case I didn't make it to the next exit with a restroom. Rolling into my home town roughly two and a half days later, I was absolutely worn out from the endless hours of sitting and driving. It was February 2nd.

After sleeping a very long night, I checked on the well-being of the person I'd received the call about. A few days later, I was able to meet her for the first time and visit for a few minutes. She was in bed, watching a show I had watched many times in the past. It seemed we had a connection. She smiled, which was nice to see. Her body was thin and frail. After the visit, I went home and cried. I didn't know that would be the one and only visit we'd have before she died.

It was a little over a week later when she breathed her last, ravaged by a disease for which no cure has been offered for over 100 years. This is despite the billions of dollars poured into the research for the most brilliant scientists in the world. Medicine, it seems, is more profitable than curing disease.

The whole happening was quick and decisive from my point of view. Her husband had searched for many years to find his perfect match. He'd finally succeeded after almost giving up hope. They were married, bought a house together, celebrated the holiday season, then death paid a visit before their first wedding anniversary. Their story still brings tears to my eyes to this day.

And the flashing red three I'd seen during the first phone call? The sense of urgency to leave? Finally, it all made sense.

Three weeks . . . She only had three weeks left to live.

11
A Chance Call

A new father, along with his wife and baby, drove to visit her family for the fourth of July holiday weekend. The dad spent that Saturday golfing with his father-in-law (and others). At some point, he became angry over comments made about a new job he was starting with a petroleum company. The dad had recently been laid off from a mining company. He called his wife from the golf course and asked her to pick him up. He told her he wanted to go back to Wyoming. While they were driving to her grandparents' house, the two got into an argument.

Once they arrived at her grandparents' house, the dad got out of the car and started walking away. Apparently he'd left in order to clear his head and calm down. As he walked, he called his family members to come and pick him up, but they were about four hours away.

He told them he wanted out of town and planned to walk 35 miles to a town in Wyoming.

He spoke with his best friend around 8:46 p.m. That call would be the last time anyone would hear from him. The last communication from his phone was a text of emojis and letters to a family member at 9:08 p.m., just as a torrential storm swept through the area. The emoji text didn't make sense to any of them (his mother said that he never used emojis). About an hour after the text, his phone went dead and he's not been seen or heard from again.

When the missing persons investigation kicked in, law enforcement obtained surveillance video that showed the man walking alone in town. He was wearing Wrangler jeans, a plaid shirt, and a trucker's cap. The video shows him looking down at his phone before taking a 90-degree turn to the left . . . as if he were following a map.

A massive search involving 17 law enforcement agencies; friends; volunteers on foot, horseback, and ATVs; drones; divers; aircraft; and cadaver dogs was conducted. The best friend said that he and other volunteers conducted about 25 searches of the area, but found no trace of his friend.

Almost five years after his disappearance, a private investigator working with his family gathered new information about his whereabouts before his phone died. A former convenience store clerk claimed to have seen the missing father in the store between 8:30 and 9:00 the same evening. He recalled the man having a "tense conversation" with another man in the back of the store prior to him purchasing tobacco and an energy drink. The clerk distinctly remembered carding the missing dad for the tobacco and the fact that he was from South Dakota. (The young father had grown up in South Dakota, and never switched his driver's license.)

The clerk recalled teasing the man about "crazy people from South Dakota" being out in a Nebraska storm. The dad then confided that he'd been in an argument with his wife and needed to take a walk, but had cooled off and was heading back now. The clerk praised him for his level-headedness in handling the situation. As the clerk rang up his purchases, the man the dad had been talking to in the back of the store was being helped at a second register by a co-worker. The clerk saw the other man hop into an unidentified vehicle, but couldn't provide details of what it looked like. He also didn't see if the missing dad got into the vehicle with him or took off on foot. He was too preoccupied with the sudden storm rolling into town.

A second new lead came in after two witnesses came forward. They recalled two beautiful women (in their mid-twenties) running alongside a road around 9 p.m. The women were in a state of distress/panic, frantically calling out for assistance, and attempting to stop traffic. The location was within a mile of the store (new location) in which the young dad was allegedly last seen. The witnesses then saw the women get into a white, two-door pickup that was towing a small boat on a white trailer. They seemed to know the driver.

The missing man was last seen on surveillance video walking down a local residential street on the evening of July 6, 2019. The new lead, however, places him at a convenience store in a neighboring city, about two miles from where he was last picked up on camera. What happened to the young father that night (and whether a crime was committed) remains the mystery that law enforcement and volunteer private investigators have been diligently trying to unravel for the past six years. His family and friends have continued to ask the public for help, and organized events to keep his disappearance in the public eye.

It was on a beautiful Colorado morning when the missing father in Nebraska caught my attention.

I'd just completed most everything on my daily "to do" list when my phone rang. Not expecting any business calls that day, (and not recognizing the number calling), I thought about letting it go to voice mail, but something urged me to answer the call anyway.

The woman caller introduced herself and told me she had met me at an event in Cheyenne, Wyoming. We hadn't known each other very long (less than three months). She told me that a young man had gone missing and called to see if I could help locate him or get anything that might help police.

While on the phone with her, I saw him sitting on a bench at a popular place. It seemed he liked this place (familiar with it). He was just sitting there, relaxing or clearing his mind. Lots of stuff was running through his head, like everything was simply overwhelming at that moment. The spot was bringing him some measure of peace. I felt like he knew the spot. Like he had been there before. Then, just as quickly as the vision had started, it was gone. It was like watching a movie trailer and suddenly the projector stopped working.

After our call ended, I asked God (the universe, Source) where he was located and any information that would help his family find him.

Sometime later, I received information on a location with directions to it. I called the lady I'd met in Wyoming back and gave her the information, but never heard from her again.

Perhaps the information wasn't believable or hope was still alive for his safe return at that time. I can't say for certain. Family and friends go through very challenging experiences when a loved one is missing. I know I did, but then, my family members were eventually found.

It's been over six years since I received the call about this young father. Over that time, I've received bits and pieces of information about him. While writing this chapter, I heard **he was NOT with his phone at the time of the emoji text**. One time, a song by Green Day, *Boulevard of Broken Dreams*, started playing in my head. On another occasion, the song *Moon Shadow* by Cat Stevens attached itself to this young man.

I've also seen a short video clip (in my mind's eye) of a male toddler wearing only a diaper and cowboy boots. He was a happy little tike. (There was something about being too old for training pants.) Suddenly, there was pain in my left elbow and I felt older, as if my body was beat up from work. (Also got a reference to "rodeo".)

From time to time, the man would come to mind (or I would be reminded of him) and would ask him questions about that day. In 2023, I received some information that seemed to be about the day he went missing. It was a hodgepodge of thoughts, feelings, and direct answers.

He was asking for help and peace. He stated he was "home". I asked if he was at the place where he grew up. "Gering" was his reply. I saw the toddler from the video clip again. Then I asked him if he wanted to talk about the day he took a walk to clear his head. He conveyed to me that he had made a connection at a gathering (like putting two and two together). The truth he realized from it was overwhelming. It concerned his wife and child.

Just then, I felt a lot of pain on the back of my head! It was just to the right of the little indentation at the base of the spine (pineal gland area). There was literally a hole in the back of my head! I saw it, felt it. Then I saw a blue light that penetrated the natural light. It seemed like it was dark outside and I heard, "peace" and "shot".

Next, I asked him, "Do you know where your body is located?" I received the name "Howe", then the words "brush", "unmarked", and "shallow". In my mind's eye I saw a map with the name "Gering" being shown.

Other words that came were "police", "busy", "cold", and "breeze". (It seemed like he was aware of people searching for him.) I asked if there was anything else he wanted to say, and heard "love her" and "Caroline". Not sure who he was referencing.

The overall impression I received from this man was that he was treated like he was beneath his wife (like she was the boss). She had a negative or berating way about her that directly affected his outlook on life (felt sad and trapped at times). There was someone with influence that intentionally caused him pain, disharmony, and conflict. He was being deceived for his money and what he could provide, which was never enough or good enough. It seemed everything he had (or made) was gradually taken or spent.

When all was said and done, someone betrayed him. Someone with power over him. He was tricked/deceived and this led to his death. He was "stabbed in the back" by those who knew him. He had no chance to defend himself. My conclusion (after receiving the various pieces over time) was that the young man was no longer alive.

What happened was not an accident. And finally, that his body will be found at some point.

12
Forgotten Father

Childhood was chock-full of fear and not knowing what might come next. My father was an alcoholic and a mean drunk. He was a decent man when he was sober. Trouble was, he was rarely sober for long. The family never knew what mood he would be in or what might set him off. It didn't take much for him to get into a heated argument with my mom or fly into a rage over the smallest of things. Once my dad lost his hair-trigger temper, he became violent. His methods of mayhem included verbal tirades, hurling various objects within reach, physical assault, and unhinged whippings with a belt.

The situation going on inside our home was worse than the endless bullying, fights, and ongoing racial tensions happening outside our house.

We knew what to expect once we stepped outside our door, but were never sure of what might transpire once we came back home. As kids, we became highly proficient at games like "walk on eggshells"; "make yourself invisible"; and "hide on top of the shed". These games were not fun, or ones kids like to play, but ones we played for self-preservation. This crazy life of drunk and disorderly, domestic violence, disturbing the peace, and trips to jail went on for years. Sometimes when stuff got over-the-top terrible, I'd hide way up in the tree in our backyard.

One day (during yet another domestic violence incident), my mom pulled a handgun on my father. The situation had gotten so out of hand that multiple neighbors called the police. And just like that, my mom had finally had her fill of the chaos. Shortly after that incident, we moved away from the house on Marshall Street. We didn't see our dad ever again (for our own safety) after that day. Even though (at the time) the whole thing felt like getting an early Christmas present, it was the end of family for me and my siblings. The last time I saw my dad, he was being driven away, handcuffed, in the back of a police car.

After a while, I stopped asking my mom about my dad. I grew up and started my own life. Now and then I'd wonder where he was, what he was doing, and if he'd ever quit drinking. Stuff like that.

I'd think about finding him, but then I would convince myself that he probably didn't want to hear from me. I figured he had a new life, or maybe he didn't even remember his kids. It's funny, the stuff that goes through your mind that you find out later isn't even true or half-true.

Some 40 years later (shortly after my mom's death), I discovered a copy of my father's death certificate among her important papers. The certificate read: "Cause of death: Adenocarcinoma of Lung with Metastases to Spine With Cord Compression in Mid-Thorax". In layman's terms, he died of lung cancer that had spread, wrapped itself around his spinal cord, and disrupted nerve signals between his body and brain. I hoped he hadn't suffered too long. Dealing with cancer is difficult enough, but experiencing radiating back pain, trouble walking, bladder or bowel problems, and paralysis must have been a whole other level of challenging.

To say those few moments I spent reading the document were weird, awkward, and sad would be an understatement. It was like I woke up that day and had a dad, then a short time later he was gone (with no context in between). My mind went back to the events of the last day I'd seen him. Now, there was no way to learn what his life had been like over the years.

I couldn't go back in time and get his perspective on things. No way to say my last goodbye or the words I needed to say (or so I thought). He was still a part of me, so there will always be a bond that exists beyond death. After all, your family is always going to be your family.

At some point, I got a hold of a copy of my dad's DD214 (military discharge papers). My father had served in the Army during the Korean War. Not sure if he was "in country" or saw combat, but I thought maybe it was the reason he drank. Things we experience during war sometimes hang on like a monkey on our back. Any substance that dulls the pain, silences the dreams, or stops the flashbacks becomes a way of coping. Yeah, maybe that's why he smoked unfiltered cigarettes and drank to excess.

About two years passed before I decided to track down where he was buried. An Internet search through historical funeral records revealed the answer. Then I searched the cemetery website to locate the exact spot where he had been interred so many years before. There were thousands of names listed, but it only took a few minutes to find the right section and gravesite number. With this information in hand, the time came for me to visit his grave.

Even though I didn't understand what my father went through in life, I felt the need to tell him I didn't hold any animosity toward him. To let him know I had forgiven him a long time ago.

The VA National Cemetery grounds were manicured, yet unpretentious. A mixture of upright and flat markers in a field of lush, green grass. Viewing the acreage, I could see row after row of white headstones, all in perfect formation. Almost as if the soldiers, sailors, airmen, and marines were still standing guard . . . forever vigilant. After entering this hallowed ground, the wind seemed to hold its breath. The leaves on the trees stopped their melodic rustle. The bird songs were magnified through the immense silence that permeated the area. Almost as if their voices were a welcoming tune being sung just for me.

A caretaker spotted me wandering about (looking lost, I imagine) and asked if he could be of assistance. I told him I needed help locating the section and number on the property where my father was buried. He asked me to wait a minute while he went inside the administration building. Shortly, he returned with a map that had my dad's location circled on it. He then offered to drive me to the spot in his golf cart. Once we arrived at the appropriate location, he left me to be alone to visit.

My plan was to simply tell my father the thoughts I'd never been able to say while he was alive. But there's a saying about the best-laid plans . . .

As I was fumbling around, trying to find the words to say to my dad, the atmosphere changed. My "Spidey sense" automatically kicked in and I diverted my attention to my surroundings. The birds had stopped singing and chirping. The wind had remained calm. The leaves on the trees made no sound. Scanning the area, I didn't see any other people around. The whole place had gone silent!

Not sensing any danger, I proceeded to tell my father the thoughts I'd had about him. I let him know I held no hate in my heart for him and that I had forgiven him ages ago. It was then I heard a man's voice say, "I'm sorry."

Even though I hadn't heard him speak in decades, I knew it was his voice (albeit when he was a bit younger). I thanked him for the apology. He told me he was sorry for his children having it so rough growing up. Never being able to see or visit us after he went to jail was always something that bothered him. He also acknowledged that his drinking and abuse were what caused him to lose his children, but said he had a "sickness" he wasn't ever able to beat.

He wanted me to know that he loved all his children and made me promise that I would tell them what was said on that day.

Before our conversation was over, I told him that I loved him and thanked him for speaking with me, allowing me to start the grieving process, and have some of my questions answered. He told me he loved me and was willing to help me if I ever needed it. The last statement felt like he was saying goodbye or "see you later", so the conversation came to an end. As I was walking back to my car to leave, the birds continued their chirps or songs. The wind began moving the leaves on the trees again.

I've not returned to visit his grave since that day. We are at a good place now in our relationship. If I ever need help in the future, or just want to have a chat, all I have to do is return to that place where heroes (and the long-suffering) rest.

13
Places of Healing

Our hospitals are designed to be places of healing. People feel comforted and trust the medical professionals who provide them with the care they need. Its walls are painted in shades that evoke a sense of healing, calm, and hope. Polished floors with multicolored lines lead us to our destination within a sometimes massive structure. The halls seem to stay forever busy with visitors, nurses, doctors, and patients coming and going. People bringing flowers or other gifts to their loved ones having to stay for surgery or recovery. There's always a chapel, adorned or simple, where prayers are sent to the heavens in askance that a loved one return to wellness.

Of course, we know people die at these healing centers. We don't really talk about it, or know when it happens . . . unless it happens to someone we know (or we're close by when another family is told of the passing of their loved one). All in all, the hospital is a tolerable (if not pleasant) experience for most people. They hope no one they love has to spend a long time there, or, God forbid, require emergency, life-threatening treatment.

I wish this near-idyllic impression for everyone, but know from experience there are many whose experience can be quite different. For some, hospitals are a scary place, filled with smells, sights, and impressions beyond what others may experience. For those whose spiritual gifts have reawakened, medical facilities can be traumatic, especially if they've not learned to protect themselves from getting sensory overload.

For me, hospitals have a distinct smell that varies only slightly from facility to facility. This smell is distinct from nursing homes, long-term care, or hospice facilities. Maybe it's the disinfectant and sterilization products they use. Perhaps it is a combination of those mixed with pain, worry, and fear. Strong emotions can have a smell. Maybe it's more of a vibe or juju the emotions leave hanging in the air.

This vibe can make your entire body feel on edge . . . sweating . . . feeling like you desperately need some fresh air. Your body becomes heavy and your energy drains quickly. You may wonder why a visit makes you feel sort of not well yourself. It's not all in your head. People pick up on things whether they know it or choose to acknowledge it.

The forming of my beliefs about hospitals began with my experiences at a young age. Due to a birth defect, I had multiple surgeries on my eyes as a child. Even at such a young age I was already awkwardly aware of my spiritual gifts. It seems these two things somehow were the catalysts for my present-day relationship with not only hospitals, but also medical facilities in general.

As best as I can recall, before my surgeries, I just "knew" things and would hear things (as I mentioned in the Preface). After the surgeries, I also began to see things. It's not a big leap in logic that correcting my vision helped this gift along. I can't tell you how or why, but that was the timing of it.

Based on my experiences at medical facilities, coupled with my "paranormal" gifts as a psychic medium, I avoid hospitals whenever possible.

Yes, I will go and visit a friend or loved one who's been admitted, but do my best to stay healthy so I don't have to be placed in care.

When I do visit, I make sure to set my intent for the visit and say my prayers before going inside. This helps me filter out those sensory impressions that are not for me to be concerned with. The only information I receive is anything that will help me with the visit, or something I need to do during my time there. This ensures my visits are stress-free (for the most part).

Just to give you an idea of my hospital experience, let me share with you what I can "get" while visiting or receiving care . . . The older the building, the more activity there usually is. Various floors and departments (specialty clinics) put off their own vibe or impression. A range of feelings, visions, or emotions can be felt just walking from one section or floor to another.

Maternity is fresh with hope and love. Newborn babies are scented with a strong vibration of their innate spiritual knowing. They've yet to go through their domestication and lose their unconditional love and joy. Delivery is tense with the pain and trauma of birth, cyclically washed away by joy and promise.

PLACES OF HEALING

The NICU (Neonatal Intensive Care Unit) smells of unconditional love mixed with a fear of survival or mortality.

Hospice feels like a wet blanket wrapped around me and smells of despair. Patients and loved ones resigned to the doctor's determination of "there's nothing more that can be done". (Even when it's not yet their time.) Relief from this daily vigil may be short-lived, or drawn out over a period of weeks or months. Depression hangs heavy on the patients and their family (like a dark cloud). But it also can be felt on the staff. Sometimes angels or loved ones come to visit (or hang out) when it's about time for their loved one to pass on.

The ER (Emergency Room) is filled with high levels of anxiety and stress. The adrenal system is working overtime. At times, the human brain cannot comprehend what is or has happened. Even the medical staff are pushed beyond their limits. It may start to feel more like a mental health facility (as the mind is pushed, at times, beyond its limits). A fog hangs over the area and if I walk into it unprepared, I'm hit with a rollercoaster of emotions, sights, and smells.

Generally, the patient floors seem to be the least active as far as sights, smells, or emotional upheavals.

However, there may be spirits of deceased patients roaming the halls or hanging out in a certain room. When this happens, I may see a figure out of the corner of my eye, or run into cold spots that send a chill down my spine. (Of course, this can be true for the entire hospital.)

The cancer wards or clinics feel a lot like hospices, but there's still an air of hope and willingness to fight the disease. Chemo drugs and radiation exposure seep from the pores and breaths of the patients. The depth or severity of the sickness is palpable in the air. Fear still sticks to loved ones, but they believe the treatment will work and remission is in the future.

Diagnostics (CT scan, MRI, X-ray, etc.) is sterile, uninviting, anxiety provoking, and not good for the body (contrast dyes and radiation). The feeling is, "I really don't want to go in there". Other than this, diagnostics is a "quieter" place compared to other areas of medical centers.

The morgue (or a room where a patient has died and has not yet been removed) is unique. There is a still finality to the air . . . mostly. It feels like the essence of the person(s) no longer exists. An empty, sterile feeling that has a silence to it, even when staff are present and working.

At times, the presence of spirits is palpable (feeling like you're not alone, someone is watching you, or the room being crowded). Perhaps they are being shown (or learning of) their death. Most seem to move on quickly, but others do not. Maybe the ones walking the halls lingered too long after death, couldn't accept their fate, or didn't want to leave for a variety of reasons.

The chapel has its own vibe, depending on the general religious theme, colors, seating, and more. A mixture of peace, bargaining, grief, and prayer swirls around its rafters. Spirits (deceased patients) pop in and out as well. Maybe they were devout to their religion in life and find a sense of peace there. Perhaps they come to comfort their loved ones before or after their passing.

There are also angels, guardian angels, Archangels, guides, and more throughout a hospital. "You are never alone" is in full effect here. I tell people all the time they have their own "posse" that supports them every single day of their lives. These beings gather and assist, however they can. From the newborn to the elderly, they are always there . . . helping. Helping with the healing and grieving process.

So, if you ever feel the hair stand up on the back of your head, drained of energy, cold spots, or you see/hear things while in a hospital, know that you're not crazy! You're just picking up on what's there . . . spirits, energies, guides, and angelic beings.

14
An Amber Alert

In early June of 1995, a mother and her six-year-old daughter attended a Little League baseball game at a local park. It was a perfect time in this small Arkansas town for outdoor activities. In June, the full, sweltering heat and humidity famous in the south hadn't yet reached their peak. After watching the game for a while, the little girl asked her mother if she could catch lightning bugs (fireflies) with her friends. The mother was uncertain, but eventually let her go and play.

The game ended shortly thereafter, but the little girl's friends came back without her. They told the mother she was at the mom's car, but when the mom went to her car, her daughter wasn't there.

Her friends remember seeing her emptying the sand out of her shoes by her mom's car while the rest of the group of friends did the same a few dozen feet (11 m) away. They also reported seeing a "creepy"-looking man talking to the girl as she was putting her shoes back on.

Other people attending the game observed a man watching the girl as she was playing with other children. A witness also saw a red Ford pickup truck (with a short wheelbase) and a white, ill-fitting camper parked nearby. The same truck disappeared about the same time as the girl. The vehicle was believed to have an Arkansas license plate and damage to the right rear area.

The creepy-looking man was described as Caucasian, six feet (1.83 m) tall, with a medium build, mustache, and a one-inch (2.54 cm) beard. He was believed to be 23-38 years old.

Within a 15-minute window, this young girl was abducted by an unidentified man and whisked away to an unknown location!

The massive investigation that ensued turned up thousands of leads, but no solid clues to the whereabouts of the young daughter or her abductor.

There were numerous possible sightings of her across the U.S. over the years. In 2002, police received a solid tip, which led them to a piece of land in Arkansas where they searched for a buried body using a police dog and other tools. The search came up empty.

In 2010, federal investigators searched a vacant house in Oklahoma, looking for DNA evidence. They returned to the same house again in 2017, using cadaver dogs which alerted on a well on the property. No evidence was found. As the years passed, all law enforcement could do was continue to investigate any new leads or tips.

A new development came in 2021, when police named a person of interest in the investigation. Unfortunately, the suspect had died in prison in 2000. The red pickup truck he drove had been the focus of their investigation since the beginning. The FBI stated that fibers found in this truck were a close match to the Girl Scouts T-shirt she had been wearing the evening of her abduction.

In 2024, the local police chief stated they had a "significant development" in the case, and a press conference was held the following day. They announced that new DNA evidence linked a member of the family to the interior of the red truck once belonging to the suspect.

They also stated the lab report "strongly indicated that the little girl had been in that truck".

After 30 years, the case of this little girl remains open and she's still listed as missing.

Having experienced part of my family going missing many years ago, I was familiar with the Amber Alert System. The first time I heard one for Arkansas, I wasn't sure why it had a different name than other states where I'd lived. So, I looked up the history and discovered it was named after this little girl who was taken against her will at the baseball game. I read the story about how she went missing and the exhaustive efforts over the years to find her. It was a sad, seemingly never-ending story and I felt bad for her family and friends, and the community.

Early on, after discovering and reading her story, a snapshot of a man's mid-section flashed in my mind. He was wearing jeans and on his belt was a large belt buckle (similar to the ones awarded as prizes to rodeo winners). I got the impression he had lived in a state with a rodeo-type culture. The feeling of cowboys, rodeos, cowboy hats, chaps, bulls, and broncs came to my mind.

During 2016 and 2017, I would experience multiple "run-ins" with this child, almost as if she was asking me to find her. On my lunch breaks, I would go for short walks to stretch my legs and get some fresh air. On one occasion, while walking back to my building after a walk, I happened to glance down at the row of newspaper boxes that were a permanent fixture there.

A "local happenings" type paper caught my eye with an age-progressed photo of the missing little girl. She wasn't little anymore, but the first time I had saw her was from a photo at the time she went missing, so she'll always be the little girl to me. I pulled a copy of the newspaper out of the box and read her story again. The paper was helping keep her story alive by printing an article about her abduction on the anniversary of it.

A short time later (while on yet another daily walk), I saw one of those billboard trucks down the street, heading in my direction. As it came closer to me, I felt time slow down. I looked to my left toward the moving vehicle, and there she was! A ten-foot (3.05 m) tall version of the missing girl looking directly at me! The mobile billboard showed an age-progressed missing poster and a number to call if anyone had any information on her whereabouts.

Have you ever looked at a painting or portrait and the eyes seemed to follow you as you moved past it? That's what this moment was like. Her eyes stayed locked on me the whole time she was rolling past. It was almost like she had become a real person, looking out from the flat screen in which she'd been placed. I stopped walking and followed her stare until her image was too far away to see. As I turned back to continue my walk, time sped up and returned to normal once again.

Sometime later, I received a vision from the point of view of someone driving. It was like I was the person driving. This person took an exit off a freeway named "Pecos Street" (Oklahoma). This vision told me the girl had been taken across state lines into a neighboring state. During that paranormal experience, I also heard, "something being hidden to this day". My overall impression was that she was taken against her will over a distance. The person who took her was prepared and ready (his intent was to find a child that evening). He knew where to look for children (this told me he was familiar with the area). Entering her space uninvited . . . he influenced her behavior by charm . . . then took her and left quickly.

All of these psychic impressions came prior to the new developments in 2021 and 2024. I did not forward these to law enforcement as I felt they weren't specific enough to be used as solid leads. For example, without a specific description of the belt buckle, how would law enforcement tie it to a specific person? Also, how many rodeo winners had there been over the years leading up to the abduction?

Perhaps in the future, more details will be disclosed and I'll be able to discern if any of the clues I received would have helped law enforcement had I revealed them.

15
The Vietnam Veterans Memorial

The grounds at our state capitol are well maintained, with native tree-lined walkways, ornamental landscaping, and lush, green, manicured lawns. In the spring, one can visit the Rose Garden and take in the lovely scents of hundreds of various types of roses. The large magnolia trees are a sight to behold when their large flowers bloom and the sweet aroma fills the air. Depending on the amount of time one has for one's lunch break or visit, it's easy to spend an hour or more strolling the grounds.

The front and sides of the Capitol building are dotted with various statues, memorials, and monuments dedicated to historically significant events and Arkansas residents who helped shape its history.

They speak of their brave actions and sacrifices in defense of human rights, our state, and the nation. Citizens can observe the statues, sculptures, and inscriptions to learn about the stories behind the Little Rock Nine; Fallen Firefighters Memorial; Vietnam Veterans Memorial; Medal of Honor Memorial; Law Enforcement Officers Memorial; Gold Star Families Memorial Monument; Confederate Soldiers Monument; Ten Commandments Monument; American Revolution Bicentennial Monument and Fountain; and more.

The Vietnam Veterans Memorial is located on the southeast corner of the grounds. Its circular design in dark granite reveals the name of every citizen (a total of 645) of the state who forfeited their life in a war which lasted over ten years. Walkways lead from it in several directions. As one approaches the monument, we notice how different it is from the other features that dot this grand parcel of ground.

It's not sweet, like the scent of the magnolias in bloom. Nor is it awe-inspiring, like the Little Rock Nine remembrance. It is somber, quiet (even amidst the backdrop of traffic), and eye-opening at the rows and rows of names inscribed on its walls. One could be taken into a state of reverence if one makes time to fully appreciate the images, shapes, and what is written there.

I'd walked the Capitol grounds many times as part of my daily work break. Given a piece of blank paper and a pen, I could probably draw a map from memory and show someone the best scenic routes and the longest or shortest walk times. The secret parking spaces close in and the best lot to park for big events. I had visited this particular memorial numerous times and always sent respect to my fellow veterans whose names were inscribed there as I passed by on my walks. Little did I know today's visit would be unlike any I'd had in the past.

As I approached the memorial, the urge to walk around the circle which encompassed the memorial came to me. I slowly traveled the circumference once, twice, then three times. After a few minutes of going round and round, I lost count of the number of times I circled slowly, not knowing what was going on or what else might happen. After the first few rounds I felt like praying, so I did. I prayed for all those whose names were emblazoned on the cold granite stone. Prayed they had found peace. Told them they were remembered by their families, friends, and fellow Arkansans. Let them know they were loved and free.

As my prayers subsided, I sensed a number of presences. Maybe a few of the fallen were here, my logical mind chimed in.

Could it be the presence of loved ones or friends who had lost someone and were drawn to this place? Before my brain took over, I focused back on my prayers, which turned into prayers of askance. I asked any relative of those named here to be present if their loved one was still walking this area. That these ancestors make their presence known to them and aid them in moving on.

Calling upon Archangel Michael and the Band of Mercy, I asked that they please come to this place now and assist any souls remaining here to move on IF it was for their Highest Good and the good of all concerned. I continued to speak aloud to any spirit stuck in that place, letting them know they were free to go. Telling them they were no longer bound to that place. Instructing them to see their Ancestors and angels that had come to escort them Home. Letting them hear that they are loved. I continued to encourage them as I walked the circle time and again, sending love, healing, and permission to them as I went.

After a few minutes, I sensed a whirling motion spinning counterclockwise (like a dust devil or waterspout). It almost felt like the spirits were being carried upward and released from their confines. A sense of release then filled the area. Then, a peace descended upon that place.

At that moment, I knew one (or more) spirits had joined their Ancestors and were no longer bound to the monument! I started to cry and thanked their loved ones for encouraging them. I thanked Archangel Michael and the Band of Mercy for assisting in moving them on from this time and place. The whole experience was so beautiful and moving. I felt the love and peace that now filled the space. It gave me comfort to know my brothers were finally at peace . . . and free.

Continuing my walk back to my workplace, I took it slow and easy. I needed time to compose myself. Not sure how long the calming feeling of love and peace lasted, but it didn't go away that day. Needless to say, I wasn't 100% at work, so I hid out in my office space . . . wanting the natural high to last as long as possible.

16
Who Killed Kenny?

Hot Springs, Arkansas, sits at the southeastern edge of the Ouachita Mountains. It was named after the natural thermal water that flows from 47 springs in the area. Every day, about one million gallons (3.8 ML) of water flows from these springs from the western slope of Hot Springs Mountain. The water is a mildly scalding 143 degrees Fahrenheit (62 degrees Celsius). For centuries, the water was believed to have curative properties. Back in its heyday, people would flock to the area for "the cure" for a variety of ailments.

Today, this small town is a national park and tourist destination. The western slope of Hot Springs Mountain sits in its historic downtown area. Bathhouses, shops, and museums based on area history fill the tree-lined streets.

Historic (and infamous) hotels form the outer perimeter. A tourist can experience soaking in the "healing" waters, a spa day, or a night-time ghost tour. Like many cities, Hot Springs has a not-so-stellar past. Illegal gambling, prostitution, and other crimes are baked into its history.

Another seedy aspect to the illegal activities of the time was rumors of underground tunnels used to move people, money, and other illicit items. These rumors were not unfounded. A tunnel was built beneath the streets of Hot Springs in 1884. The stone arch aquifer, made of granite and novaculite stone, was designed to carry excess water from bathhouses, manage stormwater, and flood control. It extends for about two miles through the downtown area.

Over the years since its construction, the tunnel became the subject of urban legend. The legend was (and still is) it was used as a secret passage by Al Capone and other mobsters during the early 20th century. It allowed them to move undetected between the Arlington Hotel and the downtown nightclubs, brothels, and gambling establishments. As the city was a Mecca of organized crime during that time, the stories aren't without merit. All the events and shady characters of the time contribute to the tunnel's mystique.

Today, the city seems (on the surface) like a totally different place than what is depicted in its history. If you walk the streets on any given day, you'll see lots of visitors popping in and out of the shops and museums. The primary street (Central Avenue) stays busy and congested, especially during tourist season. But, if you pay attention, you'll get the gut feeling that there's something else . . . just below the surface . . . just beyond the storefronts and Bathhouse Row.

That "something else" reared its ugly head one late spring day in 2009. A man was walking home from a trip to the grocery store. Carrying his three bags of groceries, he decided to take a shortcut through a vacant lot to his home. He never made it back to his house. Only a few minutes later, he was ambushed and murdered.

Not long after the incident, Hot Springs police answered a call about a white male lying in a field. When they arrived, they found the body of the man less than two blocks from his home. He had been shot in broad daylight in the sometimes deceivingly safe, tourist destination of "Spa City".

That man was the son of my mom's best friend. Our two families had pretty much grown up together. We had a lot of adventures as kids (and got into our share of trouble).

It's like we had two moms and extra brothers and sisters. After his childhood "adopted family" heard the news of his brazen murder, we were in shock. His mother, sisters, father, and brother were grief-stricken. The thought of his mother having to bury her child was beyond heartbreaking.

Like most people, attending funerals or viewings is not one of my favorite things to do. But our families had years of shared history. Although it had been quite a while since I last saw him (and we probably wouldn't have recognized each other if we passed on the street), I attended his services to support his mom and siblings however I could.

Everything seemed normal (albeit uncomfortable) as I greeted the family members and offered a handshake or hug, and my condolences. From there, I waited in line a few minutes to view the son and say any last words. As I stood in front of his casket, I no longer recognized the ever-present fixture that was part of my (and my siblings) growing-up years. After contemplating what to say, I decided upon letting him know he was loved and that his mom had a lot of people supporting her. I told him he didn't deserve what had happened to him and we would do our best to make sure those responsible were brought to justice.

Having said my last words, I seated myself in a pew to wait for the service to begin. While waiting, I observed the other mourners as they made their way through the receiving line and passed by the open casket. It was all a very quiet and somber experience . . . until it wasn't.

Out of nowhere I heard, "____ did it!" in a somewhat loud and agitated voice. I froze, exhaled slowly, then focused on everything that was going on around me. Time had NOT slowed down (which was new for me in this context). Scanning the room, I noted the service was continuing as before. Then I turned my head ever so slowly to see if anyone was seated behind or near me. No one was there. Once I realized I was indeed alone, the hair on the back of my neck stood on end. As soon as my brain registered the situation I was in, I heard it again. "____ did it!"

It was the same voice I'd heard the first time. At that moment the full realization of what was going on hit me. A spirit/ghost was talking to me in real time and telling me who killed the man whose funeral I was now attending! Holy sh*t! My brain quickly began trying to put all the puzzle pieces together. Who might be talking to me about his murder? I hadn't heard his voice in many years, so that was of no help. Was it one of his ancestors? Some random spirit that had witnessed the event?

Getting nothing that made sense, I changed my approach back to spiritual and asked who it was speaking to me. The impression I received was that it was **him**! His body was lying in the casket in the front of the room, but his spirit was behind and to the side of me, letting me know who had killed him!

Sitting there in stunned silence, I contemplated what to do with the information I'd been given. Not wanting to cause a scene, I decided to keep it to myself for the time being. The son was not happy with my decision and expected me to tell someone. In the middle of his funeral, I'm arguing quietly with him about how inappropriate it would be for me to walk up to a family member and say, "I just talked with your son and he told me who killed him."

As our disagreement continued, I reminded him of how his acting before thinking used to get him into trouble when we were growing up. His mom didn't believe in this type of stuff, so I told him I wasn't going to upset her even more by telling her about our conversation. At that point, he seemed to accept my reasoning and knew I wasn't budging on my decision. (Being the catalyst for a bizarre funeral fiasco that gets recorded and posted to social media, which then goes viral on a video titled *Funerals Gone Wrong 12* wasn't my idea of a good decision.)

After the service, I told my sister what had happened. She then approached one of the more open sisters and suggested that she hear me out. I then told his sister what I'd heard and who had told me. It seemed she believed me, but wasn't sure what to do with the message. At the time, I felt I'd done all I could do without creating a circus out of a day of grieving. I silently told the son, "I've done all I can do."

Six or seven years pass. While at work one day, the thought of him and his case popped into my head. I texted my sister, asking her if she knew whether or not his murder had ever been solved. After waiting a few minutes, she responded that no, his case was still unsolved. Checking the Internet for updates on his case, I discovered two men had been arrested and charged with first-degree murder a little over four years after his death, but were later released.

I thought how sad it must have been for the family to not yet know the truth. His mom had been through a lot and deserved to have some type of closure. No sooner had those thoughts crossed my mind than I began to receive information about his case! Turns out that his case had come to my mind for a reason. The son had knocked on the door of my awareness and I had answered. He started speaking to me once again.

What felt like a "download" of names and information started coming through me (another first). I began texting everything I was getting to my sister and telling her to forward them to his sister.

My texts to her were sent fast and furious, leaving virtually no pause for replies. In reality, I was actually channeling the brother. I was aware of what was going on, but the brother was the one actually sending the texts. For verification, he mentioned the childhood nicknames of his sisters (which I'd forgotten). He told me the same name he'd mentioned years before at his funeral.

After the download, I promised him that I would get the information out to help solve his murder. His sister said she would bring the information up to her mom. The next day, I filled out a contact form with the police department and sent it to their detectives.

Later on, his sister shared that their mom didn't believe what I had shared with her daughter, even after he used his sister's childhood nickname in the communication! I never received any response from the police department in that city. I understand why the mom and police were skeptical. They want solid evidence/proof that comes from believable sources. But I heard it all, plain as day, from the murder victim himself!

A short time later, I told him I'd done everything I could. I asked him to stop bugging me (yeah, he was hanging around) as I couldn't make people listen or believe. His voice went silent on that day. I've not heard it since. At that point, I believed it was up to God and the universe to make something happen if it was meant to be. There was nothing left for me to do.

Fast-forward another seven years or so. His story, the unfinished one, comes to mind yet again. I wonder if he's restless, wandering about, or still seeking justice. He sure didn't seem (back then) like he was settled on where he was supposed to go. The thought came to me to ask about his case again. Here's the information I received . . .

A woman seems to be at the center of this tragedy. She "has the ear" of a man who leans toward jealousy and protector. Almost like a father figure. She can easily manipulate the people around her. The word I hear (that is used to describe her) is "fire starter".

The man who was killed was warned (has to do with the woman), but he didn't listen. He failed to see just how dangerous the situation was (didn't see the big picture). Him and this woman had an emotional relationship. Before his death it seems he was kinda hiding out or avoiding certain people because of this.

He wanted a new direction in life. It seems he was surrounded by questionable people (like those who killed him) most of his life.

Also got that a little "birdie" will sing (inform cops) about what happened that day. It seems there was more than one person involved. One of the men has a cowardly personality, but would harm another if their back was turned. The other reacts in immediate and extreme ways when pushed, and gives no thought to the consequences of his actions. He's a ghost from the murdered man's past.

The people involved came from a distance. One of the perpetrators believed there could only be one man for this woman and it wasn't the man who was killed.
(All of this was revealed to me before I found and read the 2013 article.)

The last two times I've tried to search for information on the Internet about this case, I haven't been able to find any articles about the original crime or any case updates over the years (except for the report about the two individuals arrested in 2013 and later released). It's almost like they were all "scrubbed" from the Internet! Given this city's past, it makes me wonder . . .

17
Encased in the Embankment

A young student was back home visiting her parents while on break from college. She was a vivacious 19-year-old who loved fashion, her friends, and life. Also a cross-country runner, she would train by running four miles every day. On January 10, 2002, her mother saw her sleeping on the couch as she left for work at 8 a.m. About 90 minutes later, the young woman texted her parents that she was going on her morning training run and headed out shortly thereafter.

Her father returned home at 3 p.m. to go shopping with his daughter, but she wasn't at home. She hadn't left a note or any other indication of where she had gone. The family started to worry when she didn't come home that day.

As it turned out, her parents would never see their daughter again. A young woman, with her whole life ahead of her, had gone for a run and simply vanished.

Law enforcement was contacted and a missing person report filed. An extensive search was conducted. Police questioned neighbors, her inner and outer circle, and did their due diligence. A few people had noticed her jogging at various points on her route. Several neighbors saw her around 11 a.m. close to her parents' house. A strange vehicle, and a young man talking to a jogger, had been observed, but no one witnessed her actual abduction. It was as if she simply vanished off the face of the Earth. Despite all their efforts, no trace of her was found.

Investigators conducted numerous interviews and countless follow-ups over the years. Time passed, and leads in the case slowed to a trickle. Progress was slow. There have been case updates about potential suspects, cars, and even a confession (turned out to be false). A white Trans Am caught the eye of investigators as the possible "strange vehicle in the area", but no evidence linked it to the missing woman.

Authorities and her family are still trying to figure out what happened to her to this day. The family keeps her memory alive while investigators continue their search for her.

Back in October 2013, I watched an episode of *Disappeared* that featured this young woman's story. Shortly after watching this show, I received a "download" of information about the case. The first part was a series of numbers that appeared to be highway or state road numbers. The second was a short video clip of the place where she was taken or left. In the video clip, I was visiting the location and seeing it from my perspective (like I was actually there). This is what I saw . . .

A large, built-up incline (berm or embankment) with railroad tracks on top. The tracks seemed to run 20-30 feet above the surrounding terrain. I notice an entrance to a cavelike structure beneath the tracks and within the embankment. The "cave" was hidden and couldn't be seen from the air. Looking down, I saw a break in the stream rock path that runs under it.

Next thing I know, I'm inside the cave, I turned around and poked my head out the entrance to have a better look.

Turning my head to the left, I notice the railroad tracks were present at a near distance (like a curve in the route). There was a tall, thin, white guy near the berm. Just after observing the man, I heard, "Deed, Tommy" to my left and noticed a tombstone of gray granite in the distance to the man's right.

Continuing to slowly scan more to the right, there was a huge tree, and a house to the right of that tree (on a hill). The house was slightly left of center and about 3,000 feet from the berm. More trees were dotted around the house. What stood out was the huge tree that dwarfed all the other trees on the property. Looking at the front of the house, I could see what looked to be a family graveyard (to the left and behind the house). My thought was that the original owners must have resided there from the mid-to-late 1800s.

Next, I looked outside the cave to the right. There was a white railroad sign in the shape of an "X" and an incline that started to the right of the sign. The area surrounding this structure had a lot of acreage, like it was a farm. An old "No Trespassing" sign flashed in my mind. I heard a name that sounded like "Bulcher", "Belcher", or "Bucher" Farm. (I wondered if that could be the name of the family who owned/owns the property.)

Now standing under the berm (inside the cave), I looked to my right, and saw the entrance with rays from the sun shining through its opening. The area was small, but there was more than enough room for me to stand upright. As I moved my head slowly from right to left, I took in the darkness of the cave. The soil smelled damp and the temperature was much cooler than the outside air. Looking down, I noticed small rocks, slightly larger than pea gravel, lined the floor. There were little rivulets of water coursing along the cave floor from runoff or a small stream. I saw a quick flash of a shovel going into the ground. White flowers (that appeared artificial) were just to the left of the entrance.

Once my head had turned slightly left of center, my hair stood on end. I knew the young woman was there! In my mind's eye, I saw a gold necklace in the ground under rocks and earth. Then I watched as a hand slowly pulled the necklace out of the soil. It was a design similar to a fleur-de-lis (resembling flower petals). A song started playing in my ears. I recognized it as *Save Me* by Queen. The smell of perfume filled the air and I hear, "Sweet Honesty", then the word "peace".

For a moment, I thought my visit to that place was coming to an end. After all, I'd been shown where the woman was located.

But, as I continued to turn my head to the left, a chill ran down my spine as I realized there was another woman buried there under the damp soil! Suddenly, the vision stopped. I wasn't given any information about the other woman. The entire vision had lasted less than fifteen seconds.

All this sensory-driven information was a bit overwhelming, but I quickly wrote down all the details. After looking at my notes, doubt started creeping into my mind via my logical brain. "Does this state even have a highway or state road with these numbers?" I asked myself. "Are there really these features and landmarks close to her final resting place?" I wondered.

Desperate for validation, my next step was to bring up a road map of the state to verify the road numbers that supposedly went south and east. They were there! (Oh my God!) Then the town named in my download (Livingston) appeared as I followed the last road east. Switching to satellite imaging, I discovered the train tracks that led through that city and followed them to a couple of locations where the berm-like structures could be located! I wasn't able to determine the height of these structures with a ground view.

It was all there. Everything I had seen/heard in my download, I had found! The only thing I wasn't able to do was verify what lay in the small cave beneath the railroad track embankment. Online maps would be of no help in removing soil so as to uncover the remains, the necklace, or the <u>second</u> set of remains!

I wondered if the killer had found a perfect spot to hide the women he killed. The built-up area wasn't a spot where trains would stop unless there was some sort of accident or mechanical problem at that exact spot. It was far enough away from the house on the hill that any smell probably wouldn't be noticed. If someone happened to catch a whiff of the smell, they would probably assume it was a dead animal, as the house was in a rural area. It seemed the old homestead was no longer occupied and the land was not being used by whoever inherited it from their family. (Not sure how that occurred to me.)

Over a period of three or so years, I received the same video clip twice when asking about her case. The second revealed more details than the first, but the original details never changed.

While writing her story, I received more tidbits of information. The first being "more", as in there are more bodies there now than when I received the second download.

The original owners of the property were from 1763. I heard the name "Jessie". (I wasn't told if the name was of the property owner, perpetrator, or one of the victim's.)

I sent this information (except the 2023 and 2025 additional information) to the investigating agency shortly after I received it.

The case remains unsolved.

18
Capitol at Seventh

One of the benefits of working at the State Capitol Complex was the availability of a safe and beautiful place to stretch your legs, feel the warm sunshine on your face, and breathe in the fresh air. After working in a fluorescent-lit building for hours, the outdoors offered a much-welcomed break. In the spring and fall, employees and visitors would often take their lunches outside and sit on the grass or the occasional park bench.

The Capitol grounds are filled with hedged walkways and paths that criss-cross between memorials, monuments, and a virtual arboretum of plant life. Within its lush, green landscaping one can experience 37 varieties of trees (including the rare Japanese magnolia, purple leaf plum, and Arkansas Black apple).

The rose gardens boast 1,500 rose bushes, with 50 varieties that bloom throughout the summer (including the English rose and hybrid tea roses). The scent of rose and magnolia blossoms that fill the air as each blooms is soothing to the soul.

At least two times a week I would use my lunch break to take a stroll through the rose garden or get in a decent cardio workout by briskly walking the paths around the capitol. On one such late spring day, I had just walked past the Vietnam Veterans Memorial when I heard tires screeching and more than one loud bang. As I turned my head to look back toward the intersection I'd just passed shortly before, I felt time slow down.

Two or three cars had been involved in an accident. Other drivers were stopping, leaving their vehicles, and going over to check on the people involved in the crash. There was a man on his cellphone calling the emergency number for assistance. (He could have been talking to a friend for all I knew. I couldn't hear his conversation, I just "knew" he had called for help.) Everything was happening in slow motion, like at half the normal speed of life.

When I looked back at the cars involved in the wreck, I felt the presence of spirits and also "saw" them in my mind's eye. Lots of them!

Some were a white color that seemed to glow. Others were see-through, like what we'd imagine a spirit looks like. I also felt as if some of the people there (that I <u>could</u> see) were not in the physical, merely taking on that form for a time. There were other presences there as well that I felt, but did not see. Some were surrounding those involved in the accident, giving them comfort. Others were close to the people rendering aid or assistance. When I say there were lots of them . . . they were all over the place!

It seemed like they had all swooped in as the accident unfolded. From my point of view, the empty space around all these people was full of spirits and other beings. I recognized some of the spirits as the guardian angels of the drivers, passengers, and emergency personnel involved with the accident. <u>How</u> I recognized them, I can't say for sure: I just did. There were also relatives (ancestors) of the people involved in the wreck there giving comfort to the injured or scared.

I could also see/feel the guides of all the people as well. The whole scene was full of these helping spirits! Luckily, I didn't see or sense the presence of Archangel Azrael (sometimes called the Angel of Death), so I knew no one had died in the crash. Not that his presence would have been ghastly.

On the contrary, it would have meant there were casualties and he came to assist the grief stricken. Silently, I gave thanks that everyone was okay.

Standing there for a few moments (in awe of what was being shown to me), the beauty of the moment brought tears that streamed down my face. I felt I was in the presence of the All Good, All Holy, and All Love at that moment.

As soon as I recognized the gift I had been given in those moments, time sped up again and returned to normal. I continued my walk with a smile on my face, a blessing in my heart, and salty tears continuing to run down my face.

What I witnessed must be what goes on every time one of us is in danger or something bad happens. I was comforted by what I sensed and reminded (in real time) that we are never alone.

19
Life's Memories Lost

Relationships between mothers and their children can be difficult. With my mother, there were years where we didn't speak to each other. She always seemed critical of anything I chose to do in life. Honest conversations with her were almost non-existent and frustrated me to no end. Our entire relationship felt like something stuck up my bum that stiffened my spine. She could only be taken in small doses.

My mom and I went through a lot of crap over the years. Our relationship was like a rollercoaster ride I didn't buy a ticket for, had no want to go on the ride, but had to strap in for it regardless. When she became sick, I still moved back home to help take care of her. After all, she was my mom despite all the other stuff. On a selfish note, I didn't want us to be sideways when she passed.

Having known the guilt (and unrelenting grief) of words unsaid, and deeds undone, I was determined not to go through it again.

About five years after I moved back home, my mom passed away. Her body shut down due to advanced Alzheimer's and dementia. We watched her slowly deteriorate before our eyes. Experiencing the retrogression of a person unfold (and not being able to do anything to help them) is the worst. Her disease slowly erased everything she'd ever known.

My mom's life memories were the first to fade. In the end-stage, she forgot how to walk, talk, drink, eat, swallow, and even breathe. In some ways, it seemed a kinder death, because she didn't know she didn't remember, and her mind was stuck in a happier time in her life. A time when her grandkids were young, her mom and dad were still alive, and none of her children or grandchildren had died. The hardest times for me were when she forgot my name, her first-born passed and I couldn't tell her, all the trips to the emergency room, and the "Barney Fife Day".

The Barney Fife Day came a few days after they had rushed her to the emergency room because her kidneys were failing.

The doctors rehydrated her, got the infection under control, pumped her full of nutrients, and changed the medications she was on. A couple of days later, I went to visit her at the nursing home and she was awake, alert, sitting up, a smile on her face, and talking to another lady!

The Andy Griffith Show was on TV, and Barney Fife was acting goofy as usual. I asked her if she liked the show and she said, "That Barney Fife is always so funny!" I asked her if she knew her name. With a big smile on her face, she told me her name! She hadn't known her name for some time and I was floored. For a long time, she had been listless and immobile. She still didn't know who I was.

That moment felt like I was in an episode of *The Twilight Zone*. I sat with her for a while (enjoying her moment of clarity), then went out to my car and cried. Later, I would recognize this moment of clarity as a phenomenon that happens shortly before someone dies.

When I visited her a few days later, she was back to being bedridden and incoherent. Once again, I thought I might lose my mind. Was I on a virtual reality ride that transported me in and out of an alternate universe or timeline? Nothing was making sense. I was simply a spectator, powerless to effect any change or ultimate outcome.

After that visit, I sat in my car and cried again. In a text to my sister, I said I didn't know how much more I could handle. My brain was no longer adapting to this extended rollercoaster ride I'd been on for over five years.

After her latest trip to the ER, her doctor recommended putting her in a hospice. He told the family there was nothing more that could be done. My siblings and I contemplated this new choice (and its consequences) for about two weeks. During that time, we were faced with the reality that our mom wasn't going to get better. None of us wanted her to continue suffering. Maybe we didn't want our own agony and helplessness to continue either. Placing someone into hospice is a life-altering decision with no "take-backs". When all was said and done, we moved her to hospice care.

Once our mother was placed in a hospice, we knew she didn't have long to live. We contacted family members and encouraged them to stop by for a last visit with her. It was a Thursday morning when the hospice nurse called to inform me that my mom had little time left. I left work and spent the afternoon and early evening with her. The rest of the day, I talked to her and cried. I surrounded her with a pink light to let her know we loved her. Asking the angels to help her go quickly to The Light.

Her breathing was labored. I couldn't do anything except watch it happen.

Not long into this visit, I felt the atmosphere change and switched my awareness to determine what was going on. That's when I felt the presence of Archangel Azrael (Angel of Death) and our ancestors making their way to The Doorway to greet her. I wanted to do something for her, so I prayed for her speedy journey to The Light and called the horses (like I had done for my nephew) to give her a swift ride to the Other Side. At some point, a sense of peace came over me.

Wanting to do more for her, I gave her the gift of song. I sang patriotic songs like *America, the Beautiful* and holiday songs like *Silent Night* and *Joy to the World*. Some country songs came to my mind, and I sang them as well. I hummed a lullaby for a while. I sang every song I could think of (including some old Irish folk songs). The last song I sang to her was *Country Roads* by John Denver. I thought she'd like it because it talked about going home and simple life stuff, like where she grew up. After several hours I was tired, and the songs stopped coming to me. I went home to rest.

My phone rang early the next morning, before sunrise. It was the hospice nurse letting me know my mom appeared to be taking her last breaths. I woke my brother, and we rushed out the door. In my mind I was saying, "Hang on, Momma, I'm coming!" because I wanted to tell her goodbye and didn't want her to die alone. Then the thought, "No, don't hold her here!" came to me. Right then I told her, "It's okay, Mom. You go whenever you want. We'll be okay, and we love you."

My brother turned on the radio in his truck as we headed out to the nursing home. The song that had been playing was ending. The next song that came on was *Country Roads* by John Denver! I let my brother know I hadn't heard that song in ages, but I had sung it to our mom the previous night. (This "coincidence" didn't register in my brain at that moment.)

Once we arrived at the nursing home, the staff told us our mother had passed away. They were getting her ready so we could see her. We were too late to say our last goodbyes and ensure she had loved ones by her side when she died. Since I had told her it was okay for her to go when she was ready, I didn't lay any guilt on myself over it. It comforted me to know we had really said our goodbyes the night before.

Although I wanted her to have loved ones with her, I think she did (as she already had one foot on the Other Side when I was with her the previous evening).

I asked the nurse what time they pronounced her, and she told me. Later that day, I checked my phone to see what time the nurse had called. I wanted to know the approximate time I had heard the John Denver song. It was the same time my mom had died! The epiphany hit me just then. She was crossing over and sent me the song, letting me know she was going Home, "Take me home, country roads". It was also letting me know she had heard everything I'd talked about and every song I'd sung to her the night before.

My mom died at sunrise on a Friday morning the week before Thanksgiving. It was a beautiful sunrise! The sky was brilliant with red, orange, and blue hues cast upon the clouds. Multicolored autumn leaves were lit up from the sun's rays. The leaves reminded me of the changing seasons, all things returning to Earth, and new beginnings. As I took in the beauty that celebrated her Going Home, I remembered the time she visited me in Utah and asked me to sing an Irish song at her funeral. The song I sang was a folk song titled *The Green, White, and Gold*. (One of the songs I had sung for her the evening before she passed over.)

The weather was cool and cloudy (with misting rain) the day of my mom's funeral. I said to my sister, "It's going to be sunny." She gave me a skeptical look, but I knew the sun would come out and the rain would stop. I couldn't bring myself to wear black to the funeral, so I chose a light-colored dress suit. My eulogy was short, and I followed it up with the Irish song I had promised to sing for her years before. It was a wonderful service. Many people said nice things about her. Her favorite songs were played, and a montage of photographs viewed from her life. It felt like I was an observer instead of a participant.

The misty rain continued as the line of vehicles made their way to the memorial park to lay her to rest. All the mourners were waiting in silence until they placed her coffin in the mausoleum. Once placed, the graveside services would end. As my mom's coffin was being lifted and placed inside the mausoleum, the gray clouds parted and the sun came out! I looked at my sister and said, "Told ya!"

Now that I've had time to reflect, I think the sun broke through the clouds because my mom was finally happy. She was with her daughter, parents, grandson, and her son. Once my mom's coffin was safely inside the mausoleum, the sun once again disappeared behind gray clouds.

On the first anniversary of Mom's death, my sister, nephew, and I visited her grave. The day was cool and cloudy, with drizzling rain (much like the day of her funeral). We placed three white roses in her vase.

After we placed the vase into its holder, the clouds parted and the sun came out! Was it simply a coincidence? I doubt it. It was a sign from our mother letting us know she appreciated the visit.

20
The Sorrow of the Red Stone

From ancient times to the present, pipestone from a Minnesota quarry has been used by North American indigenous people. For centuries, the area has been a sacred gathering place for native nations from all over North America. While collecting the sacred stone at the quarry, known enemies would not war with each other. The Dakota people called it—and still call it—Inyan Sa K'api, [the place where] they dig the red stone. The 116-acre site was designated as Pipestone National Monument in 1937. It was, and still is, a sacred place to all the indigenous peoples of Turtle Island (North America).

Pipestone is a soft, red-hued stone that is durable and handles heat well (without cracking or shattering).

Because of these properties, it is used to make ceremonial and everyday pipes. Making a viable pipe is a sacred and exact process. The pipe plays a role in everyday life, important ceremonies, navigating profound life events, and rites of passage. It is the primary source of communication between the spirit world (Grandfather, Great Spirit, God, etc.) and human beings. Each part of the pipe has a role it fulfills when the pipe is smoked, and it is always treated with reverence.

I attend a monthly meeting where various spiritual topics are presented and discussed. After one such meeting, a friend asked if he could come by my house to give me a gift. After arriving, he began telling me the story of the pipestone. He also showed me his pipe and described how to shape one and the ceremony we would do to consecrate my pipe once I'd finished making it.

After that, we went through the normal custom of receiving a gift of such importance. I was honored that he would part with a piece he had unearthed himself at the sacred pipestone quarry. He told me he had intuited that I should be given a piece. We took some photos of how to store it, herbs used, etc., so I would remember everything I'd been taught.

That very evening, I had a vision of what my pipe would look like when it was finished. It wasn't created in the typical female style, but the male version. That seemed peculiar to me, but by this time I had learned to trust what I see and know the reasons or understanding would come later. My vision also showed me the markings it was to have on the bowl and stem. I drew a rudimentary sketch of what it looked like in my vision (or mind's eye).

Within a few days, I decided to look at the stone to determine where and how to cut the piece that would become the bowl. The piece was rather large (about 2' x 1.5', or 61 cm x 46 cm) and shaped like a mountain range. When I unwrapped the piece, a sudden wave of emotion (grief) hit me! At that moment, I had no idea where it came from or why. The grief had washed over me so quickly, I didn't have time to analyze or prepare. I just began crying (sobbing) uncontrollably! The emotion I was releasing felt like a mixture of profound grief and loss.

The intensity with which it came reminded me of experiences (and their related emotions), bottled up for a long time, suddenly released without restraint. Picture a great wave (tsunami), initially being held back by a sea wall, but each wave growing in size until it breaches any barrier and the water covers everything in its path.

That's what it felt like . . . a tsunami of emotions. Had I been standing at that moment, I believe my knees would have buckled under the force of the wave.

The releasing of the grief lasted a few minutes. I was on my knees on the floor, rocking back and forth, and wailing like a banshee! I wouldn't have been able to stop had I tried.

After the crying stopped, I said some prayers for the stone and for whatever the grief release had been about. Then I spread one of the four sacred herbs above and below the stone, and covered it with the Four Directions. In my mind, I was planning on returning to the stone and extracting a piece large enough for my pipe (once I settled down from the grief experience I'd just had, and once I had sorted it out in my mind well enough to try again). Turns out, that time never came.

Over the next several months, I attempted to work with the stone, but each time I would ride the grief wave once again. The subsequent waves were not as strong or as long-lasting as the first had been, but they still left me a weak, red-faced, salty mess. What was it about this piece of stone? How could it have such an effect on me?

It didn't feel like it was one of those cursed objects you hear about from time to time (like objects taken from Egyptian tombs).

Wanting to dive deeper into this mystery, I read more on the history of the pipestone quarry. Yes, it was considered a sacred place by the indigenous people of North America. There was an agreement or rule passed down from generation to generation that was honored by all who used the quarry. Anyone who came there would not harm any others who were there . . . even people they were warring with, or sworn enemies. This agreement has never been broken between the native nations. They only extracted what they needed to make their pipe or pipes for their people. Any unused pieces were to be returned to the quarry.

This history lesson brought up more questions for my logical mind (which would run rampant if I didn't control it at times). Since the stone was sacred, was I not worthy of having it because I was not a full-blood? I concluded this couldn't be as it had been an "intuited gift", which meant there was a reason I was to have the stone. Maybe there was some sort of past-life connection with the stone and/or the quarry from which it came? If so, it's possible that the grief/sorrow stemmed from that.

Whatever the case, it was clear strong emotions were related to or attached to it.

So, after multiple attempts to work with the stone, I decided to wait until I felt called back to it. I returned the tools my friend had loaned me to cut the stone . . . and I waited. Time passed, and a couple of years later I sold my house and moved over 1,000 miles away (1,609 km) to another state. One of the items I made sure to pack was the pipestone. It sat safely under my driver's seat for the trip and was stored respectfully in the various places I lived. About two years later, a death in the family called me back to my home state. In those two years, the call to return to the stone had not happened.

Maybe I had been too busy to notice. Perhaps I wasn't listening. Who knows? I was packing everything I owned into my car for the long trip back home. I decided not to take the stone with me, but find a good outdoor home for it to rest and maybe be discovered by someone who was able to work with it. It was a decision that made me sad (and it still does while writing these words).

A friend had a sacred place near the foothills of the Front Range of the Rocky Mountains. Spiritual classes and events were held there frequently.

THE SORROW OF THE RED STONE

It had a good vibe and had been cleared/cleansed many a time by sweet desert sage. I asked her if I could leave the stone with her and she agreed to take care of it. It seemed fitting that the pipestone shaped like a mountain range would find its new home facing a mountain range. I often imagined the rays of sunset turning the stone red beneath the backdrop of the Colorado mountains. It was a good home for the pipestone, as I was unable to return it to its home in Minnesota.

After I left the pipestone in Colorado and arrived home, I thought that was the end of the story. (Silly rabbit . . . tricks are for kids.) I'm not sure, but I think the stone had impressed upon me the history of its home. Maybe when I held the stone I received a download of all the suffering, pain, and grief of the people who had visited that quarry over time. From that historical download, the story intersected with my own past life, and the memories of those times triggered the grief. It may sound crazy to some, but it's the only thing that makes sense to me. In this life, I've never visited the pipestone quarry!

One day (while at that same spiritual monthly meeting), the friend who had given me the pipestone was talking to someone, and I heard "Chippewa". After the meeting I asked him if Chippewa meant anything to him.

He said he was reading a book about pipe making and pipestone, and thought it had mentioned something about the Chippewa. He also said he had given some pipestone to another acquaintance: he had worked with his elders to make his pipe, and it was almost complete.

Anyway, as he was telling me this, I suddenly got a HUGE chill up my spine and back of my head. It was vibrating powerfully. Then something overcame me and I started crying uncontrollably! It was like I'd been hit by a big 'ole smack of grief. I put my back against the wall, bent my knees, and leaned over like I had stomach pain. The friend I was talking to held me so I wouldn't fall. Another friend came and held me from the other side and gave me a tissue.

At some point, I realized I wasn't breathing because of the intensity of the emotions gripping me. To calm myself enough to breathe, I imagined swimming with the dolphins. Going underwater gracefully, then surfacing for oxygen before sinking beneath the surface once again in a smooth, rhythmic motion. I glanced up briefly and saw a lady I've known for years, sitting calmly with her palms facing me, sending me prayers and healing energy. I thanked her with my eyes. Focusing on the dolphins, I slowly calmed down and regained my composure.

I'm not sure how long I cried, but it felt like an eternity. In reality, it was probably around five minutes.

After I had calmed down, the friend I had been talking to asked me if I had done anything about the effect the pipestone has on me. I told him I had mostly ignored it and avoided pipestone. He said something about my needing to take care of it. He made me look at him and promise to call him if I needed any help. I thanked everyone for supporting me during my random breakdown.

A few weeks later, I contacted a guy who is Native American and asked for his opinion on what might be the cause of my ongoing pipestone drama. He said I should make my pipe because it may be healing some ancestral stuff and not to worry about the color of my skin. He also said we all have things we need to do . . . we just need to do them.

Did all the effort in understanding what was going on with the pipestone work? I think it did. It's my belief that I needed to release something for myself and my ancestors. I hope I accomplished that.

The measure of my success will be known the next time the sacred pipestone comes to me.

Please Leave a Review!

Reviews really help independent authors like me!

If you enjoyed *True Stories of the Strange and Unusual*, please leave a review on Amazon (or at your favorite bookstore).

I would very much appreciate it and I read every review!

US Review: www.amazon.com/review/create-review?&asin=1737950774

UK Review: www.amazon.co.uk/review/create-review?&asin=1737950774

Can't Wait for Book 2?

If you can't wait for Book 2 of *True Stories of the Strange and Unusual* to come out . . .

Enjoy a free sneak peek by going here: BookHip.com/CSNQKTJ

Sign up and about once a month you'll get a new short story or creep-out, insider firsts, discounts, sales, Book 2 release notification, and more!

Learn more about Book 2 at: MyParanormalStories.com

Here's to more strange and unusual in your life!
De

Also By De Fletcher

Walking the Path: A Beginner's Guide to Spirituality
(Simple Spiritual Journey-Book 1)

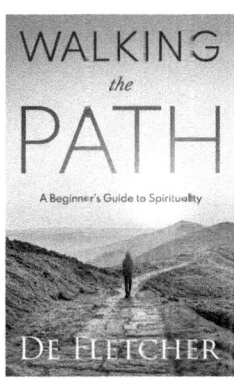

When the world seems to have gone slightly mad . . . and you feel overwhelmed just trying to live a "normal" life amidst the chaos . . .

Walking the Path will show you how to relieve the stress, drama, grief, and anxiety of daily life in our challenging world!

Whether you're a spiritual newbie or simply looking for other perspectives . . .

This simple yet powerful guide helps you:
- Quickly relieve the stress, worry, drama, or fear you experience living in today's world!
- Increase your energy, get better sleep, and elevate your mood!
- Restore your faith in "something better in life".

Plus lots more!

In *Walking the Path*, De shares simple spiritual concepts and practices based on her spiritual journey of over 20+ years. She believes spirituality is meant to be simple!

If this speaks to you on any level, buy *Walking the Path* today!

Get it in ebook or paperback from your favorite bookstore: Books2Read.com/walking-the-path

Pick up a copy at Amazon: amazon.com/dp/B0DKV7DV62

Learn more about "Walking the Path" and the author at: DeFletcherBooks.com

Born a Poor Black, Indian, White Girl
(A Memoir)

A real page-turner filled with humor, sadness, sarcasm, grief, and redemption!

It's an intense journey of hard-learned life lessons resulting from childhood trauma.

It's about how those type of experiences follow us into adulthood and the devastating affects they can have on our future.

This is one book you won't be able to put down!

De takes you on a rollercoaster ride through a traumatic childhood (and failures as an adult) that ultimately led her to a spiritual path and healing the wounds she received as a child. Keep the tissue close by!

Reading this story will make you laugh, cry, get angry, and take a deeper look into your own life.

Her stories are shared in an open and honest way, as if she were talking with a close friend. Her journey is heart-wrenching, funny, emotional, and inspirational!

If you can relate to getting over childhood scars, pick up your copy of *Born* today!

Buy the ebook or paperback from your favorite bookstore: Books2Read.com/Born

Grab a copy today at Amazon: amazon.com/dp/B07BVJD84Q

Learn more about "Born" and the author here: DeFletcherBooks.com

About the Author

De is best known as someone who picks up on things that most people don't hear or see. She has had spiritual experiences since she was a child.

The real-life stories, spiritual knowledge, and experiences she shares come from her spiritual journey over 20+ years. She has the unique ability to bring realism and humor into her books and events.

De is currently an author and speaker who enjoys solving human mysteries with both physical and spiritual tools.

Learn more about De and all her books at:

DeFletcherBooks.com and MyParanormalStories.com

Click this link to get notified when she releases a new paranormal stories book: BookHip.com/CSNQKTJ

When you do, you'll get a "sneak peek" into Book 2 of *True Stories of the Strange and Unusual*, and receive first looks, discounts, book sales, and more!

FOLLOW DE FLETCHER

On BookBub: BookBub.com/authors/de-fletcher
Be the first to know when De has a new release, preorder, or discount!

At Books2Read: Books2Read.com/DeFletcher
Click the "Follow This Author" button to get notified when I publish my next book!

Amazon Author Page:
Amazon.com/author/DeFletcher
Click the "Follow +" button to get updates on all my new books!

Coming Soon

True Stories of the Strange and Unusual (Book 2)

Are you a fan of the strange, dark, and mysterious?

If you're craving another creep-out, Book 2 won't disappoint!

More heart-wrenching to hair-raising . . . Unusual to bizarre . . . And most things in between stories!

True Stories of the Strange and Unusual (Book 2) is the continuing in-depth look into the mystifying life of a psychic medium!

Weird happenings, psychic short vids, messages from the deceased, visions, angels, visitations, time warps, and much more!

It's another wild ride filled with real-life stories of the paranormal!

Some of the stories are scary and heart-pounding. Others are eye-opening, publicly embarrassing, or send a chill down your spine!

Are you ready to step into the world of uncommon abnormality again?

If so, sign up here BookHip.com/CSNQKTJ to get notified when *True Stories of the Strange and Unusual (Book 2)* comes out!

When you do, you'll get a "sneak peek" of Book 2 and receive first looks, discounts, book sales, and more!

Acknowledgements

A special thank-you to Heather, Tammy, Melissa, Carole, Chandra, and Tonja. You guys are simply awesome!

A warm and sincere thanks to all my friends and family who continue to support my independent author career.

Thank you, Francis at 100 Covers, for the cover design.

Thank you, Matt (Editor) at ProofProfessor.

NOTE: The internet is always changing, so some of the links in this book may no longer work.

Visit DeFletcherBooks.com
 OR
MyParanormalStories.com

to be updated on any changes to the links in this book since the last printing.

www.ingramcontent.com/pod-product-compliance
Lightning Source LLC
Chambersburg PA
CBHW052204090526
44583CB00015BA/1500